Let's Be Real

Honest Discussions About Faith and Sexuality

Let's Be Real: Honest Discussions About Faith and Sexuality

(ISBN 0-687-72218-7)

EDITORIAL AND DESIGN TEAM
    Duane A. Ewers and M. Steven Games, *Editors*
    Phillip D. Francis, *Designer*

ADMINISTRATIVE TEAM
    Neil M. Alexander, *Publisher*
    Harriett Jane Olson, *Vice President*
    Duane A. Ewers, *Executive Editor, Teaching and Study Resources*
    M. Steven Games, *Senior Editor of Youth Resources*

        Cover design by Phillip D. Francis

Abingdon Press

THIS PUBLICATION IS PRINTED ON RECYCLED PAPER.

03 04 05 06 07—10 9 8 7 6 5 4 3 2

PURPOSE

To help youth, parents, and other significant adults in the church and the community have honest discussions about beliefs, values, and sexuality so that youth have guidance in their faith journey and their decision-making.

Table of Contents

Why Sexuality Education in the Church?

Introduction

The idea is not to talk *to* youth about sex but to talk *with* youth about their sexuality and their faith as incredibly powerful gifts of God.

Sexuality education in the church has many different facets. The purpose of this curriculum is to help youth, parents, and other significant adults in the church and the community develop honest discussions about faith and sexuality. Engaging youth, parents, and adults in open conversation about the topic of sexuality as a *good gift from God* is the framework for this curriculum. Using this resource, LET'S BE REAL: HONEST DISCUSSIONS ABOUT FAITH AND SEXUALITY, in conjunction with *Let's Decide: Faith and My Sexuality*, for youth, and *Let's Listen: Communicating With Your Youth About Faith and Sexuality,* for parents, opens the door to new relationships and insights.

Many different ideas exist about what sexuality education is and where it should happen. These ideas are as diverse as the people involved in the conversation. Many people say that sexuality education belongs in the home. They advocate parental responsibility for teaching children and youth about sexuality. Perhaps this would be the ideal—parents, secure in their own sexuality and trained to deal with the complexities of the subject matter, providing an open arena for discussion throughout their children's development. In actuality, research indicates that this happens in very few families. In most families, the topic is off-limits, or dealt with only in the context of issues or problems. The number of families dealing meaningfully with sexuality as both a family topic and a Christian faith issue needs to increase. Perhaps sexuality education in the church can increase the openness of communication and the accuracy of information available to families so that more faithful decisions can be made.

A majority of school systems throughout the country are now providing sexuality education for children and youth. In some situations this process has been legislated; in others, it is a voluntary response to a need in the community. While these courses have begun to include values and decision-making as a part of their curriculum, many of these education programs focus primarily on factual information. While accurate information is vital and these programs are essential, the church has a unique responsibility. The church must explore with its members and their youth what it means to be a faithful Christian as well as a sexual being. By emphasizing beliefs and values of the Christian faith, the denomination, the congregation, and the family, the church can help youth develop sound foundations for good decisions about their sexuality and behavior. Making decisions *before* situations occur can help youth live out their values, rather than reacting impulsively.

The idea is not to talk *to* youth about sex (proclaiming "Do this!" and "Don't do that!") but to talk *with* youth about their sexuality and their faith as incredibly powerful gifts of God. This curriculum will share accurate information pertaining to human development, relationships, and decision-making, all within a biblical context of the faith.

WHAT'S IN HERE?

LET'S BE REAL: HONEST DISCUSSIONS ABOUT FAITH AND SEXUALITY has been designed as a leader's guide for five ninety-minute sessions (the first five) and one two-hour session (the last session) for middle school and high school youth. Also included are optional sessions (in two different formats) for leaders to use with parents.

FAITH FOCUS

Seeing God's good gift of sexuality through the eyes of faith helps youth focus on the deeper issues of commitment, covenant, responsibility, trust, and grace. Beginning with a faith perspective sets the tone and helps youth discover the distinctive insights and concerns of the faith community.

COMMON GROUND

This section will provide basic background material for the leader. The information contained in "Common Ground" is intended to supply leaders with helpful materials not necessarily included in the session.

AGE TO AGE

Most sessions will include "Age to Age," a segment concerning specific ways this information and the activities relate to age groupings. Leaders will need to make decisions throughout the sessions about what's most appropriate for their group of youth. Options are provided so sessions can be customized to fit your group. (See Appendix A, pages 94–96, for a chart on youth development and learning sequence.)

GOD'S SAY

God's Word is central to the lives of all who are a part of the Christian community. Thus, the Scriptures are vital to our discussions on the topic of sexuality. Included in "God's Say" is the biblical information for the session, and a list of any other Scriptures that are included in the student book, *Let's Decide: Faith and My Sexuality*. This information will provide more complete understanding of the Scripture passages used in the session.

Making decisions *before* situations occur can help youth live out their values, rather than reacting impulsively.

STEP BY STEP

Teaching processes and content for the actual session with youth are found in "Step by Step." The material may contain reproducible handouts; resource lists for the session; and alternative activities for younger and older youth, when appropriate.

HOW TO USE THIS RESOURCE

SMALL GROUPS

LET'S BE REAL: HONEST DISCUSSIONS ABOUT FAITH AND SEXUALITY is designed to be used in a small-group setting. If the group grows beyond seven or eight members, participation in open, meaningful discussion becomes more difficult. Because of this, we suggest that this material be used in groups of eight or less, referred to in the sessions as family groups. A trusting, open atmosphere for discussion is essential if this curriculum is to be effective. If you  have more than eight people, you will want to divide into smaller groups.

Each family group should include both male and female participants, and an adult male and female. This allows youth to hear the views of the opposite sex and to have leadership that represents both genders. **As much as possible,** youth should be grouped according to age and development. It would be difficult for a twelfth-grade female to discuss an important dating situation with a sixth-grader in her group. Neither do sixth-graders need to be exposed to inappropriate age-level discussions.

An ideal family group might have three male youth and three female youth of roughly the same age and development along with one male adult and one female adult. Though this ideal is not always possible, balance can enhance the experience of all participants in the small-group process. **This curriculum also works better if the overall leader for the event does not also lead a small group.**

LEADING A SMALL GROUP EFFECTIVELY

PRE-REGISTRATION

Pre-registering parents and youth for this sexuality study will tell you how many leaders, study areas, and student and parent resources you need. Pre-registration will also allow you to balance the groups by age and gender, and possibly to separate cliques and couples. If you are not

Effective leadership of a small group will allow all participants to feel included and will welcome differing points of view.

planning to lead a parents' program, you may want to consider making available the parent resource, *Let's Listen: Communicating With Your Youth About Faith and Sexuality.*

ATMOSPHERE

Plan to meet in an area that suits the group and its purpose. Room size is important and needs to fit the group. If you must meet in a larger room, define your area with a rug, quilt, circle of chairs, or other method. If overhead lights are harsh, consider using lamps instead. Use posters, pictures, and other items to create a warm space. A set of ground rules, developed by the group in the first session, is essential to an atmosphere of confidentiality and trust. (See "Becoming a Group" on pages 19–20.)

SEATING

Plan to have everyone sit on the same level. If you're going to use chairs, plan for everyone to sit in chairs. If you choose to sit on the floor, have everyone join the group on the floor. Plan to sit in a circle so each person feels included and can see everyone else in the group.

LEADING

You need open, caring people who are committed to the faith and to the youth for this experience. **Leaders should be paired and should have group-building training prior to the beginning of the sessions.** This allows them the opportunity to know each other, learn about differences, and work out their team style before they meet with the youth. The following suggestions are for leaders of small groups:

▶ When all the family groups are meeting together, separate the leaders in each group so as not to overwhelm the participants.
▶ Use open-ended questions (rather than yes or no questions) to encourage participation.
▶ Use language that the participants will understand, without trying to mimic their slang.
▶ Language should be age-appropriate.
▶ Encourage more and deeper sharing by using phrases such as "tell us more about that idea" and follow-up questions.
▶ Act as the time-keeper, by limiting youth who would dominate the discussion, and by inviting others to express their ideas also.
▶ To encourage quieter youth to voice their thoughts, use this technique: When one person finishes talking, he or she invites another to speak. The other person can decline, but is given the opportunity to voice an opinion, and then asks still

You need open, caring people who are committed to the faith and to the youth for this experience.

another person to speak, until everyone in the group has been given a chance to talk.

▶ Take turns to assure that both leaders share equally in the leadership and responses.

▶ Be time-keepers for each other, allowing the group time to flow.

OPTIONS

LET'S BE REAL: HONEST DISCUSSIONS ABOUT FAITH AND SEXUALITY is designed to be used in conjunction with *Let's Decide: Faith and My Sexuality* for youth, and *Let's Listen: Communicating With Your Youth About Faith and Sexuality* for parents. While each title can be used independently, the three are more effective when used together. We will refer to these publications throughout this resource. Effectively using any curriculum requires some flexibility on the part of the leader. The youth resource was designed to be used as an individual reading resource, as well as for reinforcement of these sessions. More than likely the youth will read it in one or two sittings. You may want to adjust some activities or sessions in LET'S BE REAL to flow along with the youth resource.

Please feel free to adapt this guide.

Please feel free to adapt this guide. In situations where a learning activity or time frame does not meet the needs of the group, the leader will need to find ways to provide flexibility. If the youth are responding well to one activity and the communication is great, follow your instincts about prolonging the session, or adding another session if you have run out of time.

The parent resource, *Let's Listen: Communicating With Your Youth About Faith and Sexuality*, has six chapters, an Introduction, and a Conclusion. (See Appendix B, pages 97–103, for a study guide.)

If you are not doing all the parents' sessions at the time of your youth program, use the "Parents' Introductory Session" (See Appendix C, page 104.)

NOTE: Contact parents ahead of time about the topics for discussion in case some do not attend any of the parents' sessions.

SUGGESTED FORMATS

SIX-WEEK STUDY

Pros
▶ Time to reflect between sessions
▶ May be easier to recruit leaders
▶ May fit more easily into established structure or program

► May provide more flexibility in scheduling
► Parent's class could be held concurrently or at another time during the week

Cons
► Absences are more likely among participants and leaders
► Relationship-building may not happen as easily as with a shorter experience

WEEKEND RETREAT
(The retreat could take place in the community, with the youth going home each night; in a lock-in setting; or at a retreat center.)

Pros
► Continued involvement throughout the weekend may increase the effectiveness of the group process.
► This format may be more conducive to involving parents.
► The number of sessions and amount of time required would result in an intense experience for participants.

Cons
► A retreat away from the church may make parental involvement more difficult.
► A lock-in, or a retreat away from the church, may require leaders and youth to spend too much time on too many other details.

WEEK-LONG EVENT
(The materials might be used with youth during a week-long event in town or in a camp setting. The session material could be used in addition to other activities for the group. Another possibility would be a six-night event, with the youth going home each night.)

Pros
► More time to digest each session
► Fairly cohesive experience
► Material can be part of a structured week of activities in camp settings

Cons
► This format might not allow for parent participation as easily as other models.
► Other activities or issues may interfere with focus on the topic.

COMBINATION EVENT
(Weekly classes, culminating with a retreat for youth and parents, might be a helpful way of organizing the material.)

Pros
▶ Combines the best of both options
▶ Allows for interaction of youth and parents in a way that other models may not

Cons
▶ May be difficult for families to commit to both events
▶ May need more leaders for simultaneous groups of youth and parents

Picking and choosing from sessions will weaken the integrity of the process and the experience of those who participate.

The possibilities for using this curriculum and its companion resources are limited only by the creativity of those planning for its use. ONE IMPORTANT SUGGESTION IS TO USE ALL OF THE MATERIAL as appropriate for the ages of your youth. Picking and choosing from sessions will weaken the integrity of the process and the experience of those who participate.

BIBLICAL UNDERSTANDING
Some reasons for using Scripture in this resource are as follows:

▶ The Bible provides the source of authority for those who follow Christ. A historical appreciation of Scripture can help us understand those who wrote; those who first heard; and their time, place, and culture. (Please use the *Contemporary English Version* for all of the Scripture readings.)
▶ Helping people explore Scripture in creative ways gives them the opportunity to discover insights about God and faith related to the topic of sexuality.
▶ God speaks to us through Scripture.

Note: Be aware of the differences in language and culture that separate biblical times from present-day society. Scripture does not address the stage of development that we call adolescence. Nor does it talk about the social activity of dating. Biblical interpretation and application in these areas must be approached carefully and prayerfully.

THEOLOGICAL CONVICTIONS

▶ Sexuality is a good gift from God.
▶ Every person is a unique creation of God's.
▶ God created us male and female.
▶ God affirms our gift of sexuality and the full expression of that gift in relation to others through the covenant of marriage.
▶ God is a God of love and wants us to experience that love in all of our relationships.
▶ Grace and forgiveness are always available to God's people.

TEEN SEXUALITY RESOURCES: THE SERIES AT A GLANCE

TITLES	Let's Decide: Faith and My Sexuality	Let's Listen: Communicating With Your Youth About Faith and Sexuality	Let's Be Real: Honest Discussions About Faith and Sexuality
SESSIONS	Introduction: Just for You Session 1: Media and Culture Session 2: Anatomy and Reproduction Session 3: Decision-making Session 4: Relationships Session 5: Sexual Abuse and Misconduct Session 6: Contraception, STIs, and Safer Sex Practices	Introduction: The Most Important Person in the Room Session 1: Media and Images of Faith Session 2: Listen to Your Body Session 3: What to Do? Positive Christian Decision-making Session 4: They're in Too Deep! Positive Christian Relationships Session 5: Wait, Wait, Wait It Out! Session 6: Big-Button Issues: How Could I Possibly Talk to My Teen About That! Conclusion: Final Exam	Introduction Session 1: Getting Started Session 2: Media and Culture Session 3: Anatomy Session 4: Decision-making Session 5: Relationships Session 6: Contraception and STIs APPENDIXES A. Youth Development Chart B. Outline for Parents' Sessions C. Parents' Introductory Session D. Anatomy Model Option E. Glossary of Sexual Behaviors
SCRIPTURE	(1) Exodus 20:16 (false witness) (2) Psalm 139:9-24 (You put me together inside my mother's body.) (3) 2 Samuel 11–12:24 (David and Bathsheba) 2 Corinthians 4:7-9 (God is with us.) (4) Romans 12:1-2 (5) Luke 10:25-28 (6) 1 Corinthians 13:4-7	(Introduction) Luke 10:25-28 (Golden Rule) Genesis 1–2 (Creation/God's good gift) (1) Exodus 20:16-17 (false witness/coveting) Genesis 1: 26, 31 (2) 2 Samuel 11:2-4 (David and Bathsheba) Genesis 9:20-27 (Noah) Psalm 139 (You put me together.) (3) 2 Samuel 11:2-4 (David and Bathsheba) Matthew 5:27-28 (adultery in the heart) (4) John 4:17-18 (woman caught in adultery) (5) Genesis 39:6-7, 9 (Joseph and Potiphar's wife) (6) Matthew 23:23 (mercy, justice, faithfulness)	(1) Genesis 1–2 (Creation/God's good gift) Psalm 139 (You put me together.) (2) Exodus 20:16-17 (false witness; shall not covet) (3) John 6 (caring for the body) Romans 6:12-30 (Honor God.) Romans 12 (living sacrifice) (4) Matthew 6:33 (God's work first) Proverbs 3:5-6 (Trust the Lord.) 1 Peter 5:8 (Be alert.) (See also Genesis 2; 2 Samuel 11–12; Judges 16:4-30; John 8:1-12.) (5) Genesis 37–50 (Joseph and his brothers) Ruth 1–4 (Ruth's devotion) 1 Samuel 20 (David and Jonathan) 1 Corinthians 13:4-7 (love) (See also Genesis 25–33; Mark 6:30–44; Luke 8:26-40; Luke 10:38-42; John 4:1-26 .) (6) Romans 12:1-2 (living sacrifice)

Introduction   **11**

 # Getting Started

PURPOSE
In the context of our faith to begin to establish family-group relationships, create ground rules, and develop a common definition of the difference between sex and sexuality.

SCRIPTURE
Genesis 1–2; Psalm 139

Here's the Plan

Activities	Time	Preparation	Supplies
Nametags & Autographs, Introduction	15 minutes	Prepare nametags ahead of time. Photocopy "Autographs" (page 22).	pencils, nametags and animal stickers, copies of "Autographs"
Creation Order	10 minutes	Write Creation events on pieces of paper; make signs for Days 1 through 7.	Bible, tape, pieces of paper (construction paper will do fine) with Creation events listed, signs on walls around the room
Why Family Groups, Animal Sound Off (Use for more than one group.)	5 minutes		
Name Toss	5	Bring small ball or beanbag.	beanbag, ball, or small soft object for each group
Tangle/Untangle & Debrief	10 5		
Becoming a Group	15 minutes	Gather supplies.	large sheets of paper, markers, tape
Sex & Sexuality	10 minutes		
Worship	10 minutes	Bring Bible and goblet.	glass goblet, Bible

Getting Started

PURPOSE: *In the context of our faith to begin to establish family-group relationships, create ground rules, and develop a common definition of the difference between sex and sexuality.*

FAITH FOCUS

The lens of faith and the church's teaching are critical and central to this learning experience. In a world full of confusion and change, the church has a special role to play in providing youth with mature faith perspectives, accurate information, and effective skills to express their faith in growing, healthy relationships. Developing a sexual identity and delicate relationships with peers and family are the backdrop for helping youth think seriously and decide faithfully about God's good gift of sexuality. From the beginning it's important to emphasize that the community of faith is a safe place to explore these dynamics with other persons of faith.

COMMON GROUND

Anytime a new group forms for a common purpose, leaders need to build relationships that will allow everyone to function effectively. This is especially true if one is trying to encourage the group to communicate openly about a subject such as sexuality.

1) KNOW THE YOUTH AND THE LEADERS
Building effective groupings depends on the successful integration of all those taking part. Putting best friends or mortal enemies together in a group may keep the group from functioning in the best possible way. (Best friends have established a relationship that may prevent a group from becoming a cohesive whole.)

The same is true of two persons who are unable to get along in other settings. Parents placed in a group with their own teens may keep them from experiencing the freedom to share openly. Even having an established couple co-leading or participating in a group can change the dynamics. Deliberating carefully beforehand and seeking advice from others about persons you may not know, can make the group

Both youth and adults should make a commitment to be present for the duration of the six sessions.

participation more meaningful for all persons involved. (Remember the suggestion in the introduction about pre-registration.)

2) COMMITMENT TO THE PROCESS
Both youth and adults should make a commitment to be present for the duration of the six sessions. Absentees miss aspects of both content and group growth. Include a covenant that addresses this issue as a part of the registration process. (See sample covenant on page 23.)

3) TRAINED LEADERSHIP
Leaders should have experience in leading small groups, or training in this area should happen prior to the beginning of the sessions. Because of the sensitive nature of the subject matter, leaders need to feel as comfortable as possible with the teens, the content of the material, and the activities. It would be a good idea for the leaders to work together through all six sessions, and to preview the student and parent resources before beginning LET'S BE REAL sessions. Leaders should *always* work in pairs to assure safety and accountability for both leaders and youth.

4) MEETING SPACE
Family groups should have individual meeting spaces, which allow for privacy and confidentiality within their group. If at all possible, the same meeting spaces should be used throughout the event.

The process of group-building takes time. This session will begin with a total group and then suggest possibilities for continuing the process in smaller groups, if you are using them. Interaction will move from no-touch, low-risk to high-touch, higher-risk interaction. Allowing youth to touch in a safe environment gives them more confidence about sharing with others openly.

Gender identity, a sense of being male or female, is established by the age of five. The content of sex roles and definitions of masculinity and femininity will continue to develop throughout a person's lifetime. Media, parents, other adults, the church, and the community will have an impact on how attitudes and definitions are developed.

5) SEX AND SEXUALITY
For most youth, *sex* means "doing it." They use the term interchangeably with *sexual intercourse.* This limits the understanding of the distinctions between sex and sexual intercourse. In scientific language, the term *sex* is most often used to denote gender. Sex is a term that refers to our physical makeup as male or female. Sexuality is a term not often used by adolescents. It is, however, the favored term here because it relates to the totality of sexual expression. Our sexuality is the living out of who we are as sexual beings within the settings in which we find ourselves. A person's sexuality is part of what makes him or her unique. It includes how we look, act, and express ourselves as male or female. Simply put, our sex is our gender; and our sexuality is the expression of who we are as males and females within a cultural setting.

The process of group building takes time.

Let's Be Real: Honest Discussions About Faith and Sexuality

AGE TO AGE

Middle-school youth may be embarrassed about being a part of a program about sexuality. They are extremely self-conscious because of physical and emotional changes they are experiencing. They are curious, but may be reluctant to ask questions. Socially, they are becoming interested in the opposite sex; but they are not self-assured in their relationships. Learning happens as they experience ideas in concrete ways. They need to be able to touch and manipulate something as they learn. Spiritually, they are beginning to ask questions about religion; and they are willing to try out ideas related to the faith through stories and games. This session will give them some fun activities to begin thinking about, and chances for interacting with other participants and the subject matter.

High school youth in their mid-to-late teens are physically becoming young men and women. They probably had more input in deciding to be a part of this event. They are thinking abstractly and can manipulate ideas. They will be willing to discuss issues in more depth than will their younger counterparts. They are looking to different places for faith authority, and they want to understand what is special or unique about the Christian faith. This session can help them begin to build relationships for further in-depth discussion as this program progresses.

GOD'S SAY

The Creation story from the Book of Genesis and Psalm 139 are the passages for this session. While Genesis, Chapter 1, can be interpreted in several ways, the underlying theme is God, our loving Creator. Humanity was created in God's image. Also point out that God saw all parts of creation as "very good!" This helps establish, from the very beginning, the idea of our sexuality as a good gift from God.

The passage from Psalms reminds us that God did not create the world and sit back to watch what would happen. God is an active co-creator with us. God is involved in the creation of *every* human (Psalm 139:13-16). God knows us intimately and cares about us in ways that only our Creator can.

God is an active co-creator with us.

STEP BY STEP

Supplies
- ▶ pen or pencil for each person
- ▶ "Autographs" sheet handouts (See page 22.)
- ▶ prepared nametags
- ▶ pieces of paper (construction paper will do fine) with events of the Creation listed (See "Creation," page 17.)
- ▶ signs—"Day 1," "Day 2," "Day 3," and so on through "Day 7," on walls around the room. (See page 17.)
- ▶ beanbag, ball, or small soft object for each family group
- ▶ large sheets of paper
- ▶ markers
- ▶ masking tape
- ▶ glass goblet

Prepare the nametags ahead of time.

NAMETAGS/AUTOGRAPHS (TOTAL GROUP)
(Allow 10 minutes.)
(Use this activity if there are enough youth for more than one family group. If there is only one family group of eight youth or less, skip the animal signs on the nametags.)

Prepare the nametags ahead of time. As the participants arrive, each youth should pick up a nametag, a pencil, and an "Autographs" sheet. Along with each person's name, there should be a word, sticker, or color somewhere on the nametag, representing the family-group assignment. One easy way to do this is to write a word representing a sound or an

animal on each nametag. You can also use animal stickers. (See page 18.) When the time comes to divide into the pre-assigned groups, turn out the lights and have each person make the sound indicated on his or her nametag, until everyone has found her or his group.

Let's Be Real: Honest Discussions About Faith and Sexuality

Ahead of time, photocopy enough "Autographs" sheets (page 22) so that there is one for each youth. Give each person a sheet along with a nametag. Ask the participants to get as many autographs as possible from the others as they arrive. The idea here is to help the youth begin to be involved in conversation, while starting the process of thinking about the subject matter.

Invite the youth to sit in a circle, either in chairs or on the floor.

INTRODUCTION (TOTAL GROUP)
(Allow 5 minutes.)
Invite the youth to sit in a circle, either in chairs or on the floor. Check the "Autographs" sheets to see how many names each person has. You might ask the youth to raise their hands as you ask: "How many of you got at least 14, 10, 7, 5 signatures?" Continue until everybody in the group has raised his or her hand.

Say to the youth and adults: "Welcome to this special study of faith and sexuality. During these six sessions, we will look at our sexuality as God's good gift. We'll look at who we are as sexual beings and as God's people. We'll talk together and look at what it means to be responsible with this very special gift. We'll learn together, play together, and worship together. As we go through this program, we have the opportunity to build our relationships with one another and with God."

Desired Result
To help youth see that sexuality was created as a good gift that God has given us as a part of the whole creation.

CREATION ORDER (TOTAL GROUP)
(Allow 10 minutes.)
Ahead of time, post the signs for "Days 1–7" around the room. Ask for volunteers. Give each volunteer a piece of paper with an event of Creation described on it. Ask the remaining youth to look at the first chapter of Genesis and to help those with events place them on the signs showing the correct days that these events happened. When the events have all been placed, read verse 27 and then verse 31, from Genesis 1. Share with the youth how this version of the Creation story tells us that God very purposefully created us male and female, and that as God looked at all of creation, God thought "it was very good!"

Say: "If we believe the Genesis account, our sexuality must be a good gift from God. If our sexuality is God's good gift, then it is up to us to determine how to best use this gift."

(sample sign illustration)

Words for Events: (This is the correct order, so mix them up.)

HEAVENS AND EARTH   STARS
LIGHT   BIRDS
SKY   SEA MONSTERS
EARTH   CATTLE
SEAS   CREEPING THINGS
PLANTS   HUMANKIND
TREES   MALE
TWO GREAT LIGHTS   FEMALE

Use the nametags to get people into their groups.

WHY FAMILY GROUPS?/ANIMAL SOUND-OFF (TOTAL GROUP)

(Allow 5 minutes.)

(Use this activity only if you are using family groups. If you are using only one group, go directly to Name Toss.)

Explain the reasons for forming smaller groups:

1. So people will have a chance to get to know one another better

2. To allow for greater participation in discussion

Ask everyone to locate the word, sticker, or animal on his or her nametag. Then explain that when the lights are turned off the participants are to make the sound of the animal (or word) until they find all others in the room making the same sound. Turn the lights back on. (Group leaders should have a listing of those in their group so that they can help the youth find their assigned group.)

NAME TOSS (FAMILY GROUPS)

(Allow 5 minutes.)

Give each family group a ball; a beanbag; or a small, soft object. Have them stand in a circle facing the middle. Ask the group to give the object to the group member who has the longest hair. That person begins by throwing the ball to someone on the other side of the circle and simultaneously calling his or her name. The next person does the same without repeating anyone until each person has caught the ball. The last person sends it back to the person who started the process. Ask the groups to continue this pattern, going faster each time. When the group has done this as quickly as they think they can, have them move on to the next activity.

TANGLE/UNTANGLE (FAMILY GROUPS)

(Allow 10 minutes.)

When everyone has completed the name game, have the family groups stand in a circle facing the middle again. Ask each person to put his or her left hand into the circle, clasping the left hand of someone other than the person on either side. Then have the groups do the same with their right hand. Explain that the task is to "untie the knot" without the releasing of hands. With lots of patience and some planning, this can be done. The groups should eventually be in a circle when they are untangled. If some groups finish more quickly than others, ask them to observe the groups that are still working on the task of untangling.

When all of the groups have finished, or given up (you may need a time limit), invite them to go with their leaders to their group's meeting place.

DEBRIEF (FAMILY GROUPS)

(Allow 5 minutes.)

Have the family groups move to their meeting places. Discuss in each family group what happened during the untangling process. Use the following questions to facilitate discussion:

Everything is confidential. What is said here, stays here.

► Was it easy or difficult for your group to untangle? What made it easy or difficult?
► Did anyone take the lead in trying to get your group untangled? How did that make you feel?
► What would have made the process easier?
► What other comments do you have about the activity?

BECOMING A GROUP

(Allow 15 minutes.)

Talk briefly about being a part of a group.
► What is good about being part of a group?
► What is difficult about it?
► How is being a part of a group different from being an individual?

Say: "During this program, we will work together as a group. This will give us an opportunity to get to know one another better, and to have some friends with whom we can discuss this important subject. If we are going to have a good time together, and a meaningful time together, we need some ground rules. Let's think about what is important for us to agree on as we begin this study together."

Desired Result
To help youth experience the unique characteristics of a Christian community.

SEX	SEXUALITY

Ground Rules

Use a large sheet of paper to list the ground rules for your group. (You might ask a youth to record each suggestion.) Give everyone an opportunity to make suggestions. Ask those who do not participate for their input as well. The group will probably come up with all the ground rules that are needed; however, the following issues should be addressed in some form. Add them to the list if no one else brings them up.

► Everything is confidential. What we say here, stays here.
► Each person deserves respect.
► It is your choice to share, or to decline to comment.
► Laughter is normal, but we do not laugh at others.
► Any question is acceptable.
► Asking others personal questions is not acceptable.

When your group completes their ground rules, post the list on the wall in your meeting area.

This program gives us a chance to learn more about sex and sexuality as good gifts from God.

SEX AND SEXUALITY (FAMILY GROUP)
(Allow 10 minutes.)

Put another large sheet of paper on the wall. Draw a line down its middle. On one side of the line write SEX, and on the other side write SEXUALITY.

Say: "This program gives us a chance to learn more about sex and sexuality as good gifts from God. It's important for us to begin our study with a common understanding of these terms. Let's list ideas we have about the meaning of these two words."

After the group has brainstormed ideas about each word, use the information in the "Common Ground" section ("Sex and Sexuality," page 14) to explain how the terms will be used during this program.

WORSHIP (TOTAL GROUP)
(Allow 10 minutes.)

Bring the total group together for a time of worship. Read Psalm 139:12-16. Share with the group that we are not just the product of a biological process. God was, and continues to be, instrumental in our development. The gift of our sexuality is a special part of that creative process.

Let's Be Real: Honest Discussions About Faith and Sexuality

Pick up a glass goblet.

Ask: "What would happen if you dropped the goblet?" (You'll get different responses, but they will all have to do with the idea of the goblet breaking.)

Say: "With a delicate goblet, not only do you have to avoid breaking it on purpose, but you really need to think about it any time you handle it so that you treat it carefully. If you don't treat it with care, it might slip and break.

"Our sexuality is a gift much like a delicate goblet. It can easily be damaged, and we have a responsibility to treat it with a great deal of care. We are not like objects; we are flesh-and-blood people. You can pick up a chair and move it, turn it over, or lean back in it. You can mistreat and abuse it, and it will not feel pain. That's because the chair is only a thing. Humans were not created as things. We are important and delicate, just like the goblet. We each deserve to be treated as God's good and special creation.

"With God's love and our care, we can continue to develop into the people God created us to be. It is important to remember that even if we have been hurt and our gift is damaged, God can and will help us experience newness through God's grace and love."

Form a circle by holding hands and facing inward. Remind the youth of God's participation in our creation. Ask each youth to identify something personal for which he or she is thankful. Close with a prayer of thanksgiving for the beauty of creation reflected in each person present.

Announcements
Remind the youth about the time and place of your next meeting.

Ask the youth to bring in a CD with a song that they think reflects either a positive or a negative view of our gift of sexuality.

Our sexuality is a gift much like a delicate goblet. It can easily be damaged.

Desired Result
To emphasize again that God has created us with love and care.

Autographs

This activity is similar to a scavenger hunt. Try to find other group members who fit the following descriptions. When you do, ask each one to autograph your sheet on the line to the right of the appropriate description.

FIND SOMEONE WHO

has the same color hair as you do. _____

is excited about being here. _____

is taller than you. _____

came because her or his parents insisted. _____

is shorter than you. _____

thinks talking about sex is OK. _____

has smaller hands than you do. _____

thinks he or she knows enough about sex. _____

thinks sex is off-limits for discussion. _____

has different-color eyes than you do. _____

can think of at least one thing he or she could learn about sex._____

_____

has bigger feet than you do. _____

can define "sexuality."_____

has more hair than you do. _____

has thought about sex at least once today. _____

SAMPLE

COVENANTS

You may choose to include these items on one sheet, or combine them with other information (perhaps a medical release form if you will use this study away from home), or with the registration form, and have them signed at registration time.

Student:_____

I COVENANT to be an active part of these six sessions of LET'S BE REAL. I realize that a meaningful experience depends on my participation in every aspect of this program.

Student's Signature_____

Parents:_____

I/WE COVENANT to support our youth in their involvement in the six sessions of LET'S BE REAL. I/We will see that transportation is provided, and we will make this event a priority for our youth and our family. I/We recognize that full participation by each youth is vital to a meaningful, high-quality experience for all participants.

Parent's Signature_____

Leaders:_____

I AM COMMITTED to being involved in all sessions of LET'S BE REAL. I understand that my involvement, along with every participant's, is vital to making this a meaningful experience for all those who are involved.

Leader's Signature_____

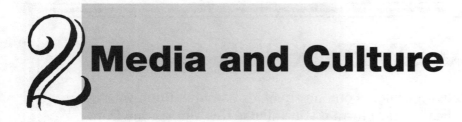

2 Media and Culture

PURPOSE
To explore the pervasiveness of media in our culture, to identify its images of sexuality, and to be clear about the counterculture images of the Christian faith.

SCRIPTURE
Exodus 20:16-17

Here's the Plan

Activities	Time	Preparation	Supplies
		Bring radio and have it playing as youth arrive.	radio/boom box
Show Time! (or Alternative)	25 minutes	Prepare a video featuring short bits of TV programs or a slide show of ads.* Create titles for each video segment; record on large sheet of paper.	large sheet of paper, VCR, prepared video
Positives & Negatives	50 minutes	Photocopy pages 31, 32, and 33. Ask students to bring CDs or tapes. Create *Positive* and *Negative* signs. Gather supplies.	photocopies, tape, markers, boom box, signs, magazines, scissors
Worship	10 minutes	Gather supplies.	mirror, chrome or silver bowl

* Federal copyright laws forbid the use of full-length films, film clips, television programs, commercials, and other material, without written permission. Before using these forms of media with your church's youth group, secure permission from the copyright holder (such as the producers of the program or the local television station).

Media and Culture

PURPOSE: *To explore the pervasiveness of media in our culture, to identify its images of sexuality, and to be clear about the counterculture images of the Christian faith.*

FAITH FOCUS

We believe the gift of sexuality is a gift from God that needs to be acknowledged and affirmed by each person, the church, and society. When we look at the wide angle of our interactions with television, movies, pop music, and the Internet, we quickly are confronted with distortions, discounted images of persons, and degrading myths about what's important. Youth learn about themselves and their world from a variety of sources. The community of faith has a crucial challenge in communicating beliefs and values based on the Scriptures and on lifestyles that clearly reflect Christ's presence in every relationship and decision.

COMMON GROUND

Sex sells! Daily we are bombarded with slogans and ad campaigns that make promises based on sex appeal. The beauty, diet, and clothing businesses are billion-dollar industries. Often the media manipulate and exploit sexuality in a way that is unhealthy and destructive. We need to look beyond the surface images to the real messages sent by media. TV, magazines, radio, music, the Internet, and other media have an impact on our attitudes and values. God's words and stories warn us to beware of false prophets, and to think carefully about the treasures we covet.

In matters of opinion and taste, our current culture is more influential than any other in history.

In matters of opinion and taste, our current culture is more influential than any other in history. The thirty-second commercial defines our self-worth. The lyrics of the current popular hit single reflect our sex appeal. The medium of TV defines what is acceptable in relationships and in social behavior. On the big screen, fleeting emotions are substituted for meaningful involvement . With the punch of a few keys, we are removed to another place where cyber relationships foster the idea that we can become whomever we choose; be both anonymous and intimate; and create an alternate reality including pictures, video, and sound.

Scientists tell us that we are shaped by two forces: our heredity and our environment. While scientists differ in their emphasis on one influence over the other, they agree that who we are is determined by a combination of the two. It would be impossible for us to look at our physical development as human beings without regard to our social development. Each force influences and informs the other. A social context is necessary to define physical beauty, relationships, what we interpret as normal and abnormal, and every other aspect of our sexuality.

How do social and cultural influences shape our understanding of God's gift of sexuality? How do we discover the good while rejecting the bad? We need to start by recognizing the real issues. We are challenged to interpret media messages in light of our personal and corporate values, rather than adopting the attitudes and values suggested by the media.

In this session, youth will begin to look critically at media and culture as they relate to God's good gift of sexuality, and at the positive and negative messages spewing forth from every outlet.

AGE TO AGE

Youth are exposed to a tremendous amount of sexual expression in the media. The values and practices represented in the media are not generally accepted as Christian, and yet they are presented as the cultural norm. Youth are likely to see casual, unprotected sexual intercourse. Violence and exploitation are often part of sexual interaction expressed in the media. Teens are treated to images of the body that can reinforce their feelings of inferiority and that may lead to eating disorders and other unhealthy practices in their search for acceptability.

Today's youth are plugged in to the computer and the Internet. Images of sexuality and chat rooms offering cyber sex (fantasy sexual experiences with someone online) are as close as the family computer.

This session seeks to help youth identify positive and negative images of sexuality in the media, enabling them to be more discerning in processing what they see and hear.

GOD'S SAY

(The Scripture given in the youth resource, *Let's Decide*, is Exodus 20:16. The first session of the student and parent resources is about media and culture. Study this verse as well as the Scripture given here in LET'S BE REAL. Also, please use the *Contemporary English Version* for all Scripture readings.)

This session seeks to help youth identify positive and negative images of sexuality in the media, enabling them to be more discerning in processing what they see and hear.

Let's Be Real: Honest Discussions About Faith and Sexuality

You may want to spend some time discussing how God's Word provides guidance for faithful living. What constitutes faithful living? How is each commandment helpful for faithful living?

In this session, the Scripture is from the Ten Commandments: "Do not tell lies about others. Do not want anything that belongs to someone else. Don't want anyone's house, wife or husband, slaves, oxen, donkeys or anything else" (Exodus 20:16-17). These last two commandments are found in the section about our relationships with others. Lying is a misrepresentation of the truth. With this definition, we can question whether the media lie to us and whether the media promote desires for things we don't need and shouldn't have. These two commandments relate to both programming and advertising in the media.

References to abstinence, the church's teaching that sexual relations are affirmed only in marriage, are included in *Let's Listen* and *Let's Decide*. Plan to discuss abstinence as a normal, valid, appropriate, healthy, and faithful choice in a culture that implies that "everyone is doing it."

STEP BY STEP

Before the session, record several video clips from TV. (This may be an assignment for one of your youth or an adult leader. Be sure you have reviewed the material together with the other leaders before it is used in the session.) Try to find messages reflecting values about sex and sexuality. Look for both positive and negative messages. Record segments of commercials, sitcoms, and so forth. Make the segments as brief as you can, while still capturing a scene. (The total tape should be no longer than about eight minutes and should contain at least five different segments.) The point of this activity is to compile a rapid-fire collection of media messages to begin the session.

Ahead of time, prepare a large sheet of paper with titles for each of the video segments. Tape the paper to the wall.

ALTERNATIVE
Put together a set of slides, or mini-posters with pictures glued to construction paper, from various forms of advertisements. The set could include magazine and newspaper ads; Web sites; billboards; bench ads; bus, train, or rapid-transit ads; displays; T-shirts; and any other form of advertisement. Put the slides together with lively music for an exciting, fast-paced presentation.

Supplies
► radio/boom box
► cassette/CD player for each family group (Group leaders might ask for volunteers to bring these.)
► *POSITIVE MESSAGES/NEGATIVE MESSAGES* signs for each family group

Compile a rapid-fire collection of media messages to begin the session.

- several CDs with current pop songs containing messages about sexuality
- masking tape for each group
- markers for each group
- a variety of magazines for each family group (especially fashion magazines)
- scissors, glue, and two pieces of posterboard or large sheets of paper for each group
- a mirror
- a silver or chrome bowl

Before the session begins, post two signs on two walls opposite each other in the room where you are meeting. One sign should say POSITIVE MESSAGES; the other sign should say NEGATIVE MESSAGES.

As the youth arrive, have a local radio station playing. Be sure it is a station that the youth in your group listen to on a regular basis. If the radio is accessible, allow them to change stations if they choose. When most of the youth have arrived, turn the music off to get their attention.

SHOW TIME! (TOTAL GROUP)
(Allow 25 minutes.)
Tell the group they will watch a video or see slides that reflect some of what we see in the media. Ask them to look for both positive and negative messages concerning our sexuality. Show the video or slides. Have a large sheet of paper on the wall with descriptive titles for each segment of the video or slides. Ask the youth to rate the different segments as positive or negative. Do this by having the youth use the room as a continuum. Designate one end of the room as the negative end and the opposite wall as the positive end.

As you call out each segment title, have the youth and adult group leaders move to a place on an imaginary line between the two ends that

reflect what they think about the segment. Ask persons at different places to discuss why they have chosen to stand in a particular place. Repeat the process through all five segments. Conclude the exercise by telling the group that the media DO send mixed messages about our sexuality, and that the session today will help us focus on some of those messages and begin to sort them out.

Direct the youth to return to their family groups and take their CD with them, if they brought one.

POSITIVES AND NEGATIVES (FAMILY GROUPS)
(Allow 50 minutes.)

This exercise provides a place for youth to experience and respond to the positives and negatives found in different forms of media. One desired outcome would be for youth to experience these different forms of media in a more critical way.

Say: "We are going to spend some time talking about positive and negative messages concerning sexuality, that you hear and see through the media."

Ahead of time, make photocopies of the CD/computer/TV handouts (pages 31, 32, 33) and have these available. Ask for volunteers to share a song from their CDs. (You will want to have several songs available too, just in case only one or two students bring CDs.)

- After playing a song, ask the group to decide what the song is saying and whether it reflects a positive or negative message about sexuality.
- On the CD handout, have a youth write the song, the message, and circle "+" or "-".
- Tape the CD handout on the appropriate wall. Do this for three or four songs.
- Tell the youth they will now think about TV programs.
- Ask the youth to consider TV programs that portray a positive or a negative view of sexuality. Give each youth and adult a TV handout and ask each person to choose a TV show to rate.
- Have the participants discuss the programs, and why they think they have positive or negative messages. Record the information on the TV handouts and hang them on the appropriate wall.

In the next activity, you will direct the students to think about computers, CD-ROMs, the Internet, and Web sites.

Ask: "How can computers help us with positive images of who we are as sexual beings? How can they cause damage with negative images?"

Use the computer handout to record the group's thinking. Hang the results on the appropriate walls, using a different sheet for each category of response.

Put a variety of magazines in the middle of the group. Ask the youth to take time to look through the magazines and to cut out positive and negative images as they relate to sexuality. When they have found a number of images, ask them to glue the pictures to two sheets—one labeled NEGATIVE and one labeled POSITIVE. When the collages are completed, tape them to the appropriate wall.

Desired Result
To encourage youth to be critical evaluators of media's efforts to shape our priorities, values, and images of others.

Give each youth and adult a TV handout and ask each person to choose a TV show to rate.

Look at all the posted sheets as a group. Which kind of messages about sexuality are in the majority—the negative or the positive? Ask the group what they think about the results of the survey.

Ask: "How do we evaluate the messages we hear and see from the media, rather than just taking them in?"

WORSHIP (TOTAL GROUP)
(Allow 10 minutes.)

Standing in front of the total group, hold a mirror so that the youth and the leaders can see themselves. You may need to walk around so that each person gets a chance to see his or her reflection in the mirror. Ask the group what they saw. They will probably respond with something about seeing their reflection. Ask them if they think what they saw was really what they look like. Next, walk around holding a silver or chrome bowl so that everyone can see his or her distorted reflection in the curved inside or outside contour of the bowl. Ask the participants how their reflection has changed. They may respond that it is distorted, messed up, and so forth.

Ask: "Which reflection is more like the reflection of life we see in the media?" Suggest that much of what we see reflects a distorted view of our world, of what it means to be human, and how God's good gift of sexuality was intended to be used. In the Ten Commandments we find this passage, "Do not tell lies about others. Do not want anything that belongs to someone else. Don't want anyone's house, wife or husband, … or anything else" (Exodus 20:16-17).

Close with a prayer reflecting our need for that which is real in our lives.

Ask: "Do the media lie to us? In terms of sexual intercourse, does everyone do it?" Ask the youth to tell why the church teaches that abstinence is a normal, valid, healthy, and faithful choice. Help the youth think about their emotional and spiritual health, the oneness of body and mind, and about the quality of relationships. Sexual intercourse is not simply a physical activity like eating. Emotionally, people can be hurt deeply by inappropriate sexual activity and can retain scars for the rest of their lives. Also remind the youth about caring for their physical health (avoiding pregnancy and STIs).

Ask the youth to consider the role of media in their life. We are surrounded by it, so we can't just exempt ourselves from it. Use a few moments of silence to allow the youth to think about their response to the media in relation to God's good gift of sexuality.

Close with a prayer reflecting our need for that which is real in our lives. Ask God to help our perspectives be more like the mirror than the distorted image in the bowl.

SONG _____

MESSAGE:

Session 2

IMAGES

Let's Be Real: Honest Discussions About Faith and Sexuality

PROGRAM _____

_____

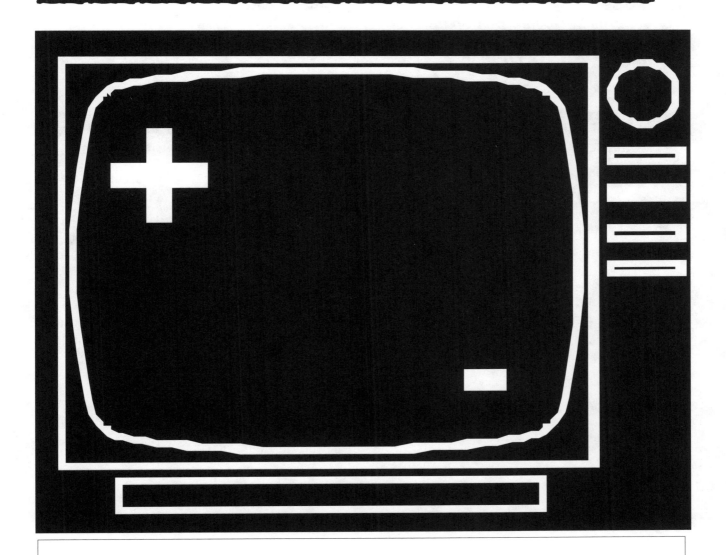

MESSAGE:

Anatomy

PURPOSE
To reinforce basic information on anatomy and reproduction as a part of the wonder of God's creation.

SCRIPTURE
John 6; Romans 6:12-30; Romans 12

Here's the Plan

Activities	Time	Preparation	Supplies
Word Picture	10 minutes	Write a different part of the body on enough index cards to give one to each person in the group as he or she arrives.	Index cards, tape
Anatomy Jeopardy	25 minutes	Write the answers in a grid on a large sheet of paper, making sure that the words are large enough to be read by the group (in some cases this might be best done with an overhead projector). Cover each answer with a separate piece of paper on which you have written the amount of points that the question is worth. See an example of a round of the game on pages 38–39.	Prepared Anatomy Jeopardy, sheets of paper, masking tape, prizes, bells
Anatomy Basics	35 minutes	Photocopy "Anatomy Basics," one copy for each student.	(See pages 42–44.)
You're the Artist	10 minutes	Gather supplies. Photocopy pages 45–52 and "Glossary," Appendix E (pages 116–117) to hand out to the youth.	Large sheets of white paper, markers, copies
Worship	10 minutes		

Let's Be Real: Honest Discussions About Faith and Sexuality

ANATOMY

PURPOSE: *To reinforce basic information on anatomy and reproduction as a part of the wonder of God's creation.*

FAITH FOCUS

A century ago, males entered puberty at age 18. Today, puberty begins at 12 or 13, a decade before most young people finish their education. Each year, millions of teens say yes at least once to sex. The church can be that place where youth feel free to learn the positive aspects of their bodies and their sexuality as gifts of God's creation. We can let youth know that we are limited in our understanding of this complex gift of sexuality and that's why it's so important to learn together. In every session with adolescents, we can share the communal challenge to find faithful, committed, and loving ways to express God's gift of sexuality.

COMMON GROUND

Why talk about anatomy in a Christian sexuality study, when we know that many youth have already participated in classes at school that deal with the material? Many youth feel uncomfortable discussing their questions, fears, and concerns in a school setting. They fear that someone will laugh at or tease them. The security of their family group gives these youth a place to ask their questions or to use the resources available to discover the answers for themselves. Also, if we are to give a *holistic view of God's creative action in our world and the beauty of all of God's creation,* including our bodies, we need to include this session in this resource. It is also important not to make assumptions about what youth know or don't know. If some youth do not have the following information and understanding, they may not participate fully in the next sessions. However, based on the understanding level of your youth, you may want to omit or adapt parts of this session.

Creating a common ground of basic information concerning anatomy and reproduction is important. For that reason, this common-ground section contains a lot of background material to provide everyone with the same information. If all of the youth and adults have already been exposed to the basics, this material can be a helpful review. If you have

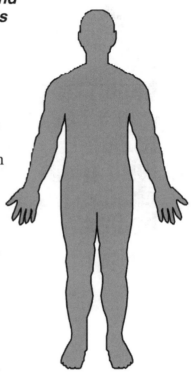

Teens' lack of assurance about their physical changes also affects them emotionally and socially.

never led a sexuality education program, the following information will help establish a foundation on which to build this and future programs. The basic information provided in this section has been designed so that each piece can be given as a handout to all participants, and it is highly recommended that you do make a handout for each person. *Let's Decide* does not include any detailed anatomy information. Reproducible pages with this information appear on pages 45–52.

AGE TO AGE

Adolescence is a time for redefining all that a person has previously accepted, while deciding on new directions that call for exploration. Dating and socializing with peers helps youth explore and understand their emerging sexuality and sexual responses. Sexuality education and sexual self-esteem development is an ongoing process of discussions, experience, and learning and takes times and patience. People who feel good about themselves tend to be more responsible in their sexual behavior. Younger adolescents will be experiencing the beginning stages of puberty. They may be experiencing physical changes that they do not understand. They can feel uncomfortable, awkward, and self-conscious. They can be emotionally unpredictable. They experience highs and lows, ups and downs, that last moments or days.

Older youth have begun to live with their changed bodies. Body image is incredibly important. Self-esteem, independence, peer relationships, dating, and sexuality are just a few of the areas that they continue to build, explore, and develop. They can react equally with an "I-know-it already" attitude or an open, receptive one.

One important factor remains on the roller coaster ride of adolescence— youth need adults who will be open and honest and who will honestly communicate about the physical and emotional aspects of sexuality.

GOD'S SAY

The Scripture given in the youth resource, *Let's Decide,* is Psalm 139:9-24. Please study these verses as well as the Scripture given below. Also, please use the *Contemporary English Version* of the Bible for Scripture readings. The third section of *Let's Decide* is "Anatomy and Reproduction."

The Bible speaks of how we are to be good stewards of our bodies. There are many examples in the Bible that teach us how we are to consider our bodies a gift from God and that we are to care for our bodies. In our faith tradition, body and soul are united—and are good.

Senior high youth have begun to learn how to live with their changed bodies.

▶ Romans 6:12-20	Honoring God with your body
▶ Romans 12	Body as living sacrifice, holy, acceptable to God
▶ John 6	Caring for the physical body

The Song of Solomon can be used in talking about the body and the unity of bodies. Some Jewish traditions held that persons were not allowed to read the Song of Solomon until the age of twenty-five, due to its explicit and graphic description of the human body. (Consider this book for a later Bible study dealing with the love and unity of two persons.)

STEP BY STEP

Supplies
- ▶ index cards and markers
- ▶ large sheet of paper for each family group
- ▶ bells
- ▶ markers
- ▶ prizes (video rental or fast-food coupons, movie passes, candy bars)
- ▶ copies of "Glossary," Appendix E, pages 116–117

WORD PICTURE (TOTAL GROUP)
(*Allow 10 minutes.*)

Ahead of time, write a different part of the body on enough index cards so that each youth can have one. Use all parts of the body, not just the reproductive system. Hand a card to each youth as he or she arrives. Ask the youth to use a piece of tape to attach their card to a blank wall in the location their body part would go. By the time everyone arrives, there should be a word picture of the complete human body on the wall.

ANATOMY JEOPARDY (FAMILY GROUP)
(*Allow 25 minutes.*)

Explain the following rules:
1. Answers have to be made in the form of a question, such as "What is *conception*?"
2. The first player to ring the bell has the right to answer the question. If the player answers correctly, he or she gains two points. If the player answers incorrectly, another player may ring the bell for a chance to score one point.
3. Prizes go to the persons with the most points.

An example of an Anatomy Jeopardy chart and its answers are on pages 38–39.

Desired Result
To help youth begin to think about our bodies and how we are created by God.

We are to consider our bodies a gift from God.

Here is an example of headings for a round of Anatomy Jeopardy dealing with the basic terms:

FEMALE	MALE	PREGNANCY	SEX/SEXUALITY	SEXUAL VIOLENCE	STIs
small, bud-shaped organ and the most sensitive part of the female genitals	organ that serves as the passageway for sperm or urine; becomes enlarged and erect during sexual excitement	tubes through which ova pass from the ovaries to the uterus	stimulating one's own genitals to experience sexual excitement and/or orgasm	sexual activity of any kind between members of the same family	life-threatening virus that causes a disease that damages the immune system (The virus is passed from an infected person's blood, mucus, semen, or vaginal secretions.)
muscular passage, three-to-five inches long, extending from the cervix to the external vaginal opening	carries the sperm to the prostate gland	when the sperm and egg unite, and the fertilized egg implants itself in the lining of the uterus	what makes you different from everyone else; how you look, act, and express yourself as a male or as a female. It's how you value, respect, and regard everything about being you.	act of violence in which sexual activity is forced on one person by another	infections passed from an infected person by means of sexual intercourse or oral intercourse
opening at the neck of the uterus	tube that carries urine from the bladder to the penis	connects the mother and fetus through their circulatory systems	sexual and emotional attraction between a male and a female	sexual contact between a child and adult or older child for the sexual pleasure of the older person	fastest-growing STI, especially among people ages fifteen to twenty-four
hollow, muscular, pear-shaped organ, where the fetus develops during pregnancy	is found along each testicle, the channel of small tubes approximately twenty feet long. The sperm cells are stored here and undergo a maturation process that takes several weeks.	acts as a buffer from noise, temperature, and physical bumps	male or female who has never had sexual intercourse		one of the most dreaded STIs, due to its longterm effects; caused by spirochete

The following are the answers to the Anatomy Jeopardy chart on page 38:

FEMALE	MALE	PREGNANCY	SEX/SEXUALITY	SEXUAL VIOLENCE	STIs
Clitoris	Penis	Fallopian Tubes	Masturbation	Incest	HIV/AIDS
Vagina	Vas Deferens	Conception	Sexual Self-esteem	Rape	Sexually Transmitted Infections
Cervix	Urethra	Umbilical Cord	Heterosexuality	Sexual Abuse	Chlamydia
Uterus	Epididymis	Amniotic Fluid	Virgin		Syphilis

Paul tells us that our entire body is important, and that each one of us is a part of the body of Christ.

ANATOMY BASICS
(Allow at least 35 minutes.)

Distribute photocopies of "Anatomy Basics" (pages 42–44) to the youth and ask them to fill in the blanks as well as they can. After a few minutes, encourage small clusters of two to three youth to work together to complete the assignment. After the clusters have had an opportunity to collaborate, spend a few minutes giving the correct responses (below), making comments, and answering questions.

Option: Do the activity "Construction of the Male and Female Anatomies," in Appendix D, pages 107–115.

Key to Anatomy Basics

1. hymen	21. sperm	41. masturbation
2. clitoris	22. penis	42. abortion
3. vulva	23. epididymis	43. sexual intercourse
4. vagina	24. scrotum	
5. labia	25. prostate gland	44. puberty
6. fallopian tubes	26. seminal fluid	45. orgasm
7. uterus	27. erection	46. sexual abuse
8. ovulation	28. ejaculation	47. HIV/AIDS
9. ovum	29. seminal vesicle	48. heterosexual
10. ovaries	30. vas deferens	49. homosexual
11. circumcision	31. embryo	50. oral intercourse
12. pubic hair	32. menstruation	
13. genitals	33. cervix	51. incest
14. breasts	34. conception	52. sexuality
15. nocturnal emission	35. pregnant	53. sexually transmitted disease
16. vasectomy	36. menopause	
17. glans penis	37. fetus	
18. foreskin	38. tubal ligation	54. anal intercourse
19. testicles	39. placenta	
20. semen	40. contraceptives	55. rape

YOU'RE THE ARTIST (FAMILY GROUP)
(Allow 10 minutes.)

The family group can be divided up into different groupings (males and females, pairs, and so forth) for this activity. Ask the participants to draw on large paper the male anatomy and the female anatomy and to label each part. When they have finished, give each person the handouts and have the group look over their drawings and the illustrations from pages 50–52. You may want to distribute copies of the "Glossary" here (Appendix E, pages 116–117).

Let's Be Real: Honest Discussions About Faith and Sexuality

CLOSING WORSHIP
(Allow 10 minutes.)

Read John 1:14 from the *Contemporary English Version*.
"The Word became a human being and lived here with us.
We saw his true glory, the glory of the only Son of the Father.
From him all the kindness and all the truth of God have come down to us" (John 1:14).

"God made it this way in the hope that creation would be set free from decay and would share in the glorious freedom of his children" (Romans 8:20b-21).

Share the following three meditations from *Meditations With Julian of Norwich,* versions by Brendan Doyle (Bear and Company, Santa Fe, New Mexico, 1983; pages 29, 95, 93). (Julian of Norwich was a fourteenth-century English mystic.)

"As the body is clothed in cloth
and the muscles in the skin
and the bones in the muscles
and the heart in the chest,

"so are we, body and soul,
clothed in the Goodness of God
and enclosed."

"Because of the beautiful oneing
that was made by God
between the body and the soul

"it must be
that we will be restored
from double death."

"God is the means
whereby our Substance
and our Sensuality
are kept together
so as to never be apart."

Encourage the youth to voice their thoughts on the meditations. Then close with prayer.

Anatomy Basics

vulva   labia   clitoris
    hymen   vagina

_____ 1. A thin membrane that may partially cover the entrance to the vagina

_____ 2. Female sex organ near the upper front of the vulva that is sensitive to touch and sexual stimulation

_____ 3. External parts of the female genitals

_____ 4. Passage leading from the outside of the female body to the uterus

_____ 5. Folds or lips of the female genitals that surround the opening of the vagina

ovaries   ovum   ovulation
   fallopian tubes   uterus

_____ 6. Tubes through which ova pass from the ovaries to the uterus

_____ 7. Place in which a baby grows until birth

_____ 8. When the mature ovum pushes through the surface of the ovary and enters the fallopian tube

_____ 9. Female reproductive cell

_____ 10. Female glands where reproductive cells are stored

breasts   pubic hair   circumcision
   nocturnal emission   genitals

_____ 11. Surgical procedure that removes the foreskin of the penis

_____ 12. Appears in the genital area of females and males at the time of puberty

_____ 13. Sex organs of the female or male

_____ 14. The mammary glands, which enlarge during puberty and are sensitive to stimulation and function to feed the newborn baby

_____ 15. Ejaculation of excess semen during sleep

Let's Be Real: Honest Discussions About Faith and Sexuality

semen   testicles   foreskin
    vasectomy   glans penis
	erection ejaculation seminal vesicle
	    seminal fluid vas deferens

_____ 16. Surgical procedure blocking the vas deferens; stops release of sperm during ejaculation, preventing conception (sterilization)

_____ 17. The head of the penis, which is sensitive to touch and sexual stimulation

_____ 18. Skin that extends over the head of the penis

_____ 19. Male glands that produce reproductive cells

_____ 20. Thick, milky substance of sperm and seminal fluid

_____ 26. Fluid that transports sperm

_____ 27. The enlarged and firm condition of the penis during sexual excitement

_____ 28. The discharge of semen from the penis during orgasm

_____ 29. Small organ attached to each vas deferens that produces some of the seminal fluid

_____ 30. Tubes through which sperm pass from the epididymis

scrotum   penis   sperm
   prostate gland   epididymis
	cervix conception embryo
	    menstruation pregnant

_____ 21. Male reproductive cell

_____ 22. Male sex organ; serves as the passageway for sperm or urine; becomes enlarged and erect during sexual excitement

_____ 23. Storage space for maturing sperm

_____ 24. Sac of loose, wrinkly skin attached to the base of the penis that contains the testicles

_____ 25. Gland that produces some of the seminal fluid and acts as a valve to control the passage of either semen or urine

_____ 31. Tiny bud of cells that form during the first stage of human development in the uterus; when organs of the body are formed

_____ 32. Periodic discharge of the lining of the uterus

_____ 33. Lower end of the uterus, opening into the vagina

_____ 34. The fertilization of an ovum by a sperm

_____ 35. The condition of a female from the time of conception until the birth of a baby

fetus   placenta   menopause
   contraceptives   tubal ligation
	sexual abuse heterosexual HIV/AIDS
	   oral intercourse homosexual

_____ 36. The stage of a female's life when ovulation ceases and hormonal changes occur

_____ 37. The body of cells in the uterus that has begun to take something of a human shape in the second stage of development

_____ 38. Surgical procedure to block the fallopian tubes to prevent conception (sterilization)

_____ 39. Lining in the uterus that provides nourishment for the fetus

_____ 40. Devices or methods used to prevent conception

_____ 46. Sexual contact between a child and an adult or older child for the sexual pleasure of the older person

_____ 47. A life-threatening virus that causes a disease that damages the immune system; passed from an infected person's blood, mucus, semen, or vaginal secretion

_____ 48. Sexual preference for persons of the opposite sex

_____ 49. Sexual preference for persons of the same sex

_____ 50. Stimulation of a person's genitals by the partner's mouth

puberty   orgasm   masturbation
   sexual intercourse   abortion
	sexuality incest anal intercourse
	   sexually transmitted disease rape

_____ 41. Fondling, caressing, and touching one's own genitals or another's genitals, sometimes to orgasm

_____ 42. Termination of pregnancy in the first 24 weeks after conception either voluntarily or naturally

_____ 43. The union of the vagina and the penis

_____ 44. A time when radical physical changes occur and the reproductive system becomes active

_____ 45. Highest point of sexual excitement

_____ 51. Sexual relations between close relatives

_____ 52. More than sex, it means all that is involved in living out what we understand to be a female or a male

_____ 53. Disease passed from an infected person through sexual or oral intercourse

_____ 54. Penetration of the anus by the penis; a high-risk behavior for the transmission of HIV

_____ 55. Forced sexual intercourse by someone known or unknown to the victim and against his or her will

Let's Be Real: Honest Discussions About Faith and Sexuality

REPRODUCTIVE ANATOMY
Glossary of Terms

Together all the female external sex organs or genitals are known as the **vulva.** The **mons pubis** is a pad of fatty tissue over the pubic bone. This area gets covered with pubic hair during puberty.

Extending downward from the pubic hair are the **labia.** The outer lips of the labia protect the vaginal and urinary openings. The inner lips of the labia are quite sensitive to touch. During sexual stimulation they swell and darken in color.

The **clitoris** is a small, bud-shaped organ and the most sensitive of the female genitals. The clitoris can be compared to the penis. During sexual excitement, the clitoris swells with blood and for most women is a center of orgasm.

The **urethra** is the external opening for the passage of urine from the body.

The **hymen** is a thin membrane just inside the vaginal opening. It may be stretched or torn during the first experiences of sexual intercourse. There is usually some discomfort, bleeding, or pain associated with this stretching. Quite often the stretching has already been done either by the use of tampons or by physical activity.

The internal sex organs are the woman's reproductive organs. The **vagina** is a muscular passage three to five inches long extending from the cervix to the external vaginal opening. The vagina serves as a passageway for the menstrual flow from the uterus, a receptacle for the penis during intercourse, and stretches during labor to allow a child to be born. The walls of the vagina produce a cleaning and lubricating fluid that also keeps the walls moist.

The **cervix** is the opening at the neck of the uterus. The **uterus** is a hollow, muscular, pear-shaped organ. The fetus develops here during pregnancy. During menstruation the lining of the uterus is discharged.

The **fallopian tubes** extend from the uterus to the ovaries. They are about four inches long. It takes an egg about 72 hours to travel to the uterus. If intercourse occurs during this period, pregnancy will likely occur if no birth control method is being used. If the sperm does not fertilize the egg, it passes into the uterus and dissolves.

The **ovaries** produce **ova** and also the female sex hormones, **estrogen** and **progesterone**. Approximately every 28–32 days an egg is released into the fallopian tube, a process called **ovulation.** At birth women are born with all of the ova they will have, between 300,000 and 400,000. Only about 300–400 ova will mature and be released. Fertilization can occur up to three to five days after ovulation.

MALE ANATOMY

The visible parts of the male sexual anatomy are the **penis** and the **scrotum.** Inside the body are the **prostate gland,** the **seminal vesicles,** and the tubes that link the system together.

The two **testes** are the male reproductive glands. They are contained in a pouch-like sac called the **scrotum,** which hangs below and behind the penis. Each **testicle** is oval in shape about one and three-fourths inches long and one inch wide. The testes produce the male sex hormone, **testosterone,** and sperm cells (approximately 500 million a day), which are the male reproductive cells. The sperm cells are needed to fertilize the egg in the female body.

The **scrotum** is divided into two separate compartments, one for each testicle. Usually the left side hangs lower than the right, and its scrotal sac is slightly larger.

The **epididymis** is found along each testicle. It is a channel of small tubes approximately twenty feet long. The sperm cells are stored here and undergo a maturation process that takes several weeks.

The **vas deferens** are the two tubes, one from each testicle, that carry the sperm to the prostate gland. They are about 16 inches long and wind upwards into the pelvic cavity. They come together and join with the urethra just below the bladder. In a **vasectomy** (contraception surgery) a one-inch section is removed, keeping the sperm in the testicles permanently.

The **prostate gland** surrounds the urethra and vas deferens junction. The sperm cells mix with the liquid in which sperm are carried out of the body, the seminal fluid. Sperm mixed with seminal fluid is called **semen.** Semen is a thick whitish fluid.

The **seminal vesicles** contribute some of the seminal fluid; the rest is produced in the prostate gland.

Let's Be Real: Honest Discussions About Faith and Sexuality

The **urethra** is the tube that carries urine from the bladder to the penis. It is also the way the semen leaves the penis. Urinary output is stopped during sexual activity by a valve system in the bladder to allow the safe passage of semen.

The **penis** is inserted into the female body during copulation. Most of the penis is made up of a spongy tissue and loosely covered with skin. The average length of a grown man's penis is between three to five inches when flaccid (not erect), and between five to seven inches when erect. There are many different sizes of penises. The size of the penis has nothing to do with sexual satisfaction or ability. The urethra enters the penis and runs inside it to the tip. The opening in the tip of the penis, the **meatus** or **glans penis,** is where semen or urine leaves the body. The **foreskin** is the skin covering the head of the penis. Often the foreskin is routinely removed at birth in a surgical process called **circumcision.**

During initial sexual stimulation, the **Cowper's gland** sends a few drops of fluid into urethra, preparing it as a safe passage for the sperm by neutralizing the acids from the urine that would otherwise kill the sperm. It is possible for the fluid to contain some stray sperm cells that can result in fertilization if birth control methods are not used correctly.

PUBERTY

The physical changes that occur during adolescence mark puberty. These changes can occur anytime during the teen years but usually occur between eleven and seventeen years of age. The physical changes that occur are triggered by the production of the sex hormones (estrogen, progesterone, and testosterone).

Some of the Changes Females Experience
► Menstruation begins.
► Pubic hair and underarm hair grows.
► Breasts develop.
► Pelvic structure changes—women have wider hips and a lower center of gravity.
► Height stabilizes.
► Weight changes.
► Hormonal changes produce a great increase in sexual responsiveness.

Some of the Changes Males Experience
► The penis, testicles, and scrotum grow larger.
► Pubic hair, underarm hair, chest hair, and coarser leg hair begin to grow; voice changes occur (usually the voice becomes deeper).

► Nocturnal emissions or wet dreams begin. This indicates that sperm are being produced and that the maturation and storage process has begun. When the storage areas are filled to capacity, emission of sperm and semen occurs naturally as a way to create more space for sperm produced daily. Nocturnal emissions have their name because they often happen at night during sleep.
► Shoulders broaden.
► There can be a height growth spurt.
► Weight changes.
► Hormonal changes produce a great increase in sexual responsiveness.

HEALTH

A **Pap smear** is a test women should have as a part of routine physical check-ups. A pelvic exam is necessary for the doctor to obtain a sample used for the test. The Pap test detects cervical abnormalities, like cervical cancer. When there is a need to repeat a Pap test for whatever reason, a wait of two to four weeks after the original test is necessary for a clear reading on the new test.

Breast self-examinations should be done monthly to discover unusual lumps that can be an early indication of breast cancer. The breast normally may have small lumps and areas that are tender, especially around the time of menstruation. Learning what your breast normally feels like will be important in detecting whether a lump is suspicious and needs medical diagnosis.

Testicle self-examinations should be done monthly to become aware of any abnormal growth. Learning what the testicles feel like and noticing any changes will be important in detecting whether a lump is suspicious and needs medical diagnosis.

Menstruation begins in females sometime between thirteen to fifteen years of age. However, there is a wide range of ages of first menstruation among individuals. Every month or so after menstruation begins, the uterus prepares for a fertilized egg. The uterine lining builds up with blood to prepare a place for the egg. If the egg is not fertilized with sperm, the lining breaks down. Menstruation is the discharge of this lining of the uterus. The fluid that is discharged contains some blood, giving the discharge a reddish color. Sometimes the lining comes away in small clots.

A recognizable pattern or cycle of menstruation is usually established for each individual. It is helpful to keep a calendar with starting dates and ending dates to help establish a pattern. Many cycles average 28 to 32 days between the beginnings of periods. The average "period" lasts between 4 to 6 days. Each woman has her own timetable. The regularity of menstruation can be affected by emotional and/or physical stress.

The menstrual flow is usually heavy the first day or two and then tapers off. Many women experience one or more of the following: cramps, back pain, headaches, water retention, feeling bloated, feeling unusually emotional, irritability, nausea, diarrhea, and/or vomiting.

During **menopause** menstruation usually ends. Menopause can occur anytime in a woman's life, but it usually occurs from around 45 years of age on.

Premenstrual syndrome (PMS) usually begins 10 to 14 days prior to the onset of menstruation and can become progressively worse until the onset or for several days after the onset of menstruation. The symptoms include the following: irritability, mood swings, bloating, cramps, sugar craving, breast tenderness, allergies, depression, weight gain, cystitis (inflammation of the urinary bladder), urethritis (inflammation of the urethra), sore throat, anxiety, headache, back pain, migraine, asthma, hoarseness, acne, fainting, joint pain, dizziness, constipation, breast swelling, infrequent urination.

Toxic Shock Syndrome (TSS) is a disease believed to be caused by toxin-producing strains of the bacterium *Staphylococcus Auras*. Seventy percent of the reported cases relate to women using tampons during menstruation. The warning signs of TSS include a sudden high fever, vomiting, diarrhea, a rash that looks like a sunburn, dizziness, sore throat, and fainting or near fainting when standing up. TSS can rapidly progress from flu-like symptoms to a serious illness that can be fatal. Teenage girls and women under 30 are at a higher risk of developing TSS. Women who use tampons should follow the instructions carefully to reduce the risk of developing TSS.

The Female Reproductive System
Vulva

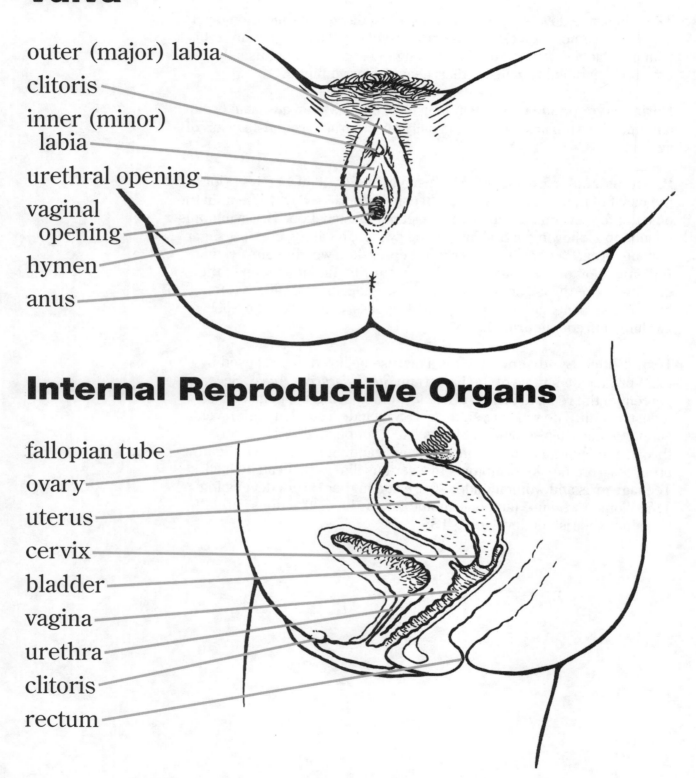

outer (major) labia

clitoris

inner (minor) labia

urethral opening

vaginal opening

hymen

anus

Internal Reproductive Organs

fallopian tube

ovary

uterus

cervix

bladder

vagina

urethra

clitoris

rectum

Let's Be Real: Honest Discussions About Faith and Sexuality

Internal Reproductive Organs
(Continued)

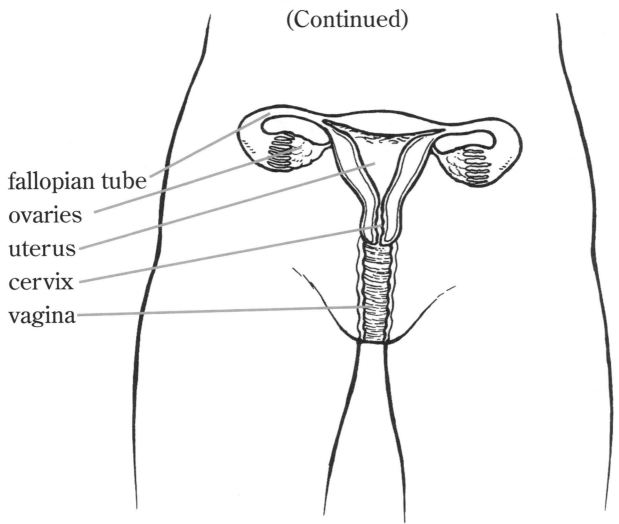

fallopian tube

ovaries

uterus

cervix

vagina

The Male Reproductive System
Genital Area

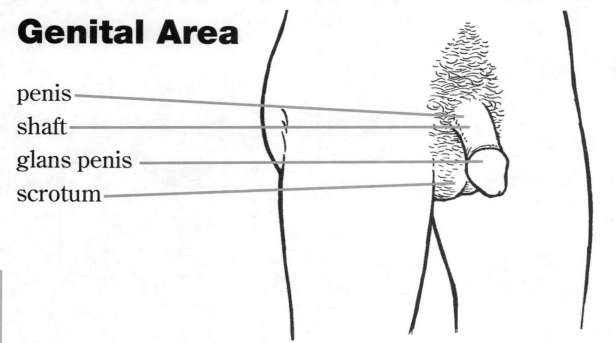

penis
shaft
glans penis
scrotum

Internal Reproductive Organs

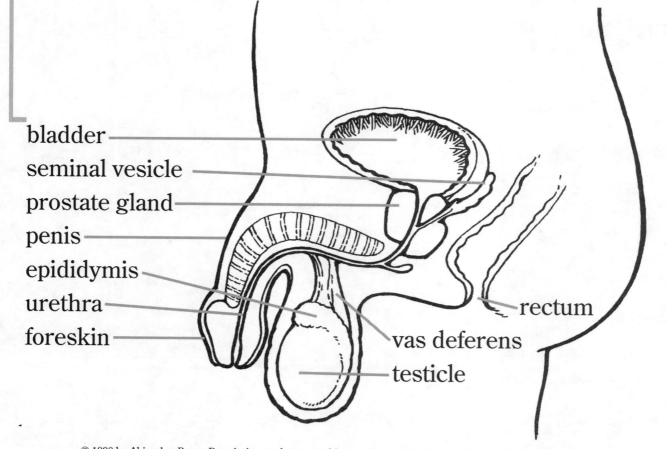

bladder
seminal vesicle
prostate gland
penis
epididymis
urethra
foreskin

rectum

vas deferens
testicle

Let's Be Real: Honest Discussions About Faith and Sexuality

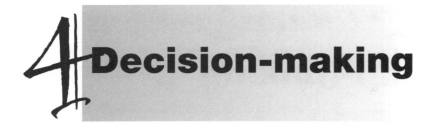

4 Decision-making

PURPOSE
To introduce decision-making models that can enable youth to make faithful decisions.

SCRIPTURE
*Genesis 2; Judges 16:4-30;
2 Samuel 11–12; Proverbs 3:5-6;
Matthew 6:33; John 8:1-12; 1 Peter 5:8*

Here's the Plan

Activities	Time	Preparation	Supplies
Bible and Decision-making	20 minutes	Study the Scriptures. Carefully read through the development and learning sequences.	Bible
Decision-making	60 minutes	Gather supplies and prepare Model 1 from pages 57–58, Models 2 and 3 from pages 58–59.	masking tape, long sheet of paper such as freezer paper, markers, index cards
Worship	10 minutes	Photocopy the litany from page 61.	litany copies

Decision-making

PURPOSE: *To introduce decision-making models that can enable youth to make faithful decisions.*

FAITH FOCUS

Teens see thousands of scenes of suggested sexual behavior during any one year of prime-time television. They receive confusing messages like "sexual intercourse is OK when you are really in love." Is "really in love" the basis for faithful decision-making? Will "really in love" keep them from emotional and spiritual harm or protect them from unintended pregnancy or sexually-transmitted infection? We, as the church, need to speak clearly to youth and help them learn to make decisions that are faith-based expressions of their highest commitments. We can encourage youth to say no firmly and know why the answer is no. Decision-making is difficult for all of us. We will not be there when the decision is made—but the sharing and modeling of our faith and values can be a part of sensible, responsible, and faithful decision-making.

COMMON GROUND

Making choices about sexuality will always be a part of life. Making those decisions can be frustrating, confusing, exciting, difficult, stressful, and affirming. Our sexuality is part of what makes us different from everyone else. It includes the ways people look, act, and express themselves as female or male. Taking the time to think about our faith, information, feelings, and attitudes is a vital first step in decision-making about sexuality.

Christian decision-making begins with God. It is the church's understanding that God wants sexual intercourse to be expressed in marriage. Abstinence before marriage is a way to protect ourselves from disease, pregnancy, and even death. But more important, it is God's desire that we protect ourselves from spiritual and emotional harm.

One of the toughest decisions youth make concerns whether to engage in sexual activity. Do they become sexually active? What behaviors and activities are appropriate? Are they ready to date? How do they treat their

Youth believe that they are indestructible, that they are immortal, or that "It won't happen to me!"

bodies? How do they know when they are in love? And of course the big question, "Do I go all the way and have sexual intercourse?"

The church believes that marriage is the covenant within which our sexual gift is best expressed. This belief calls for clear, faithful decisions.

Each teen faces these decisions and many more as he or she navigates through the adolescent years. Youth need to know that participating in sexual activity of any kind never proves their love for someone. Before deciding on sexual expressions of any kind, it is important to be comfortable with who they are, both physically and emotionally. They are not ready to do what they are not able to talk about. *Let's Decide* suggests the following two checklists that youth can walk themselves through as part of making decisions related to sexual expressions:

You are not ready if you are trying to
- ▶ prove something
- ▶ fill emptiness
- ▶ rebel against your parents
- ▶ hold on to someone
- ▶ be accepted

If you decide to express yourself sexually, be sure to
- ▶ reflect on your church's beliefs and values;
- ▶ ask yourself, "Is this something God would want me to do?"
- ▶ consider your values;
- ▶ remember that abstinence is the only true "safe sex."
- ▶ understand your motives (what are your reasons for becoming sexually active?);
- ▶ know the facts;
- ▶ consider all the possible outcomes;
- ▶ learn to show love in multiple ways;
- ▶ consider your parents' feelings, thoughts, and values;
- ▶ know what you think is appropriate behavior, what activities you are comfortable with and willing to do, and what activities are off limits;
- ▶ Ask yourself, "Am I ready for an intimate, physical relationship?"
- ▶ discuss things as a couple.

The Bible is a vital resource on how to make decisions and apply them to today's life situations.

AGE TO AGE

The ability to make wise decisions is particularly difficult for adolescents to develop for several reasons. (Refer to developmental charts in Appendix A, pages 94–96.) Some youth believe that they are indestructible, that they are immortal, or that "It won't happen to me!" They are known to challenge all adults by saying that they are able to make decisions on their own, and that they are not babies any longer. Actually, youth still look to their parents or other significant adults for guidance and boundaries, but are not willing to openly state that they continue to need their parents' involvement in their lives.

GOD'S SAY

The Scripture given in the youth resource, *Let's Decide,* is 2 Samuel 11–12:24. The third section of the youth resource is "Decision-making." Study these verses as well as the Scripture given in this session. Please use the *Contemporary English Version* for all Scripture readings.

The Bible is a vital resource on how to make decisions and apply them to today's life situations. The Old and New Testaments offer a plethora of stories of how people just like you and me made decisions and of the consequences that were involved.

STEP BY STEP

Desired Result
To help youth understand that healthy decisions are based on the Bible and the expression of our faith.

THE BIBLE AND DECISION-MAKING (FAMILY GROUPS)
(*Allow 20 minutes.*)
Ask: "How are faithful decisions made? The Scriptures offer us insights about making decisions in our life."

Read aloud the following Scriptures and discuss what is meant by them, and how they can influence youth as they begin to make healthy choices in their lives.

> "But more than anything else, put God's work first and do what he wants. Then the other things will be yours as well" (Matthew 6:33).

> "With all your heart you must trust the LORD and not your own judgment. Always let him lead you, and he will clear the road for you to follow" (Proverbs 3:5-6).

> "Be on your guard and stay awake. Your enemy, the devil, is like a roaring lion, sneaking around to find someone to attack" (1 Peter 5:8).

When working with any small group, the leader should never tower over the participants.

Questions for discussion:
▶ If you were to put these biblical statements in your own words, how would you say them?
▶ What are some reasons these insights are in the Bible?
▶ What is God asking you to do before you make a decision in your life?
▶ What will be the consequences if you do? if you don't?

56

► When life's choices get hard for you, where do you turn and why?

Other Scripture possibilities:

Genesis 2   Judges 16:4-30   2 Samuel 11–12
John 8:1-12

DECISION-MAKING (FAMILY GROUPS)
(Allow 60 minutes.)
Model 1
This first model is to be created on a LONG sheet of white paper. (Freezer paper would work well.) Every column should be covered up to the title so that the participants cannot read ahead the first time you introduce this process.

Note: When working with any small group, never tower over the participants. Either be at eye level or below them, especially in this activity, so that the youth do not feel that they are being dominated by an adult who wants to stand and lecture. If need be, get down on the floor and work there. Always remember to *stay at the participants' level and to never stand over them.*

List the following topics across the length of the paper to make a long chart that can be written on.

Discuss the following and record notes from the discussion.

ISSUE: This is the subject you are trying to decide about. Some suggestions could be whether to go to a party where alcohol is being served; whether to go all the way; or one of the suggestions on pages 59–60. Ask the youth in your family group if there is a topic that they would like to use with this model. Always use youth suggestions first.

DEFINITION: Make sure that all issue-related words listed are defined adequately. (Do we all understand what going all the way means?)

List the following topics across the length of the paper to make a long chart that can be written on.

Desired Result
To encourage youth to become aware of how they currently make decisions.

ISSUE What are you trying to decide?	DEFINE Any word that is unclear	WHO IS INVOLVED?	WHAT ARE THE CONSEQUENCES if yes? if no?	WHAT ARE THE FEELINGS you will deal with if you say yes?...if you say no?	MY STANDARDS for decision-making	WHO OR WHAT INFLUENCES	WHO FINALLY DECIDES

What can the Scriptures say to us as we seek to make decisions?

WHO IS INVOLVED? More than one person is usually involved in a decision. All parties need to be listed.

WHAT ARE THE CONSEQUENCES, IF YES? IF NO? Brainstorm the pros and cons of the issue. Sometimes the consequence will be listed as both a positive and a negative.

WHAT ARE THE FEELINGS, IF YES? IF NO? For each person involved in the decision, what will his or her feelings be (depending on the consequences that have been listed)?

WHERE'S MY STANDARD FOR MAKING DECISIONS? Do I rely on biblical mandates and images to help me decide? What kind of spiritual discipline have I chosen to guide my decisions?

WHO OR WHAT INFLUENCES? Who or what is going to influence the decision that is to be made? (Example: Parents, teachers, school, peers, the church, and so forth, could all be influences in a specific decision that needs to be made.)

WHO FINALLY DECIDES? When you have worked your way through this model, distribute index cards to everyone in the family group and ask the members to respond to four questions:

- ▶ What is your decision about anything involved in the issue?
- ▶ Who is affected by your decision?
- ▶ How do you feel about your decision?

Desired Result
To acquaint youth with options for making decisions.

Model 2
A.R.M. =
What is *appropriate* for faithful disciples?
What is *responsible* in light of all the facts we have?
What is *mutual*?
(*Mutual* means that everyone involved with the decision agrees, has thought things through, and feels comfortable).

Model 3
R.E.S.T.
John Wesley (the founder of Methodism) followed a decision-making process that is now called the Wesley Quadrilateral. This approach to decision-making suggests a balance among four areas.

Decision-making based on this model entails thinking about the issue in relation to each element of the "Quad," then how they balance. A decision is the outcome of that thinking.

REASON is the ability to use our intelligence to make a decision. What is the reasonable way to decide this issue? Our intellect is a gift from God, and we should use it.

EXPERIENCE is looking to our past involvement, or that of other people, with the issue at hand.

SCRIPTURE is our primary source for understanding faith and beliefs. What can the Scriptures say to us as we seek to make decisions?

TRADITION is what has been acceptable to the church over the years and what our particular church believes about certain topics, issues, or practices.

Briefly explain the three models that are posted on the wall. Then say: "We are going to look at some situations through the steps of each of these decision-making models."

The family group can work together, individually, or divide up into pairs. Have each group choose three situations so that they can look at a different problem with each of the models. When they have finished, return to the family group and discuss the exercise.

Questions to help the discussion:
- ▶ Which model was most helpful? Why?
- ▶ How did you use the model in helping you come to a decision?
- ▶ Tell the group about one of your situations, your decision, and how you decided that.

Decision-making "Situations"

- ▶ Steve has asked Marcia to the school dance. Marcia really wants to go to the dance. She is hoping Andy will ask her; but he hasn't, and time is running out.
- ▶ Lisa, fourteen, has been asked by Ron, seventeen, to go to the movies. Lisa is afraid to ask her parents because she thinks they will say no.
- ▶ Bill feels he may have gone too far on his last date with Tracy. He feels guilty and uncomfortable but doesn't know what to do.
- ▶ Jim is angry with his mother for treating him like a kid all the time. His buddies are going to have a party at the beach; and they've told Jim they'll fix him up with Becky, who knows how to "show a guy a good time."
- ▶ Sixteen-year-old Mary is pregnant. She is afraid to tell her parents because she knows they will be angry. She is thinking about having an abortion and not telling anyone.
- ▶ Melissa and Chris have been together for a while. They've had discussions about sex. Chris suggests, "Let's experiment to see what

it's like. If we don't like it, we'll never have to do it again. If we both agree, it will be all right."

▶ Sex is something to be enjoyed. Everyone is *doing it*. If you love the person, then being sexually active is all right. At least that's what everyone seems to be saying. But Kim and Mark don't know what they believe.

▶ Sue's boyfriend, Pete, has invited her to his house for pizza and a movie. Pete has been pressuring her lately to do more than just kiss and fondle each other with their clothes on. When Sue gets to Pete's house, she discovers that his parents are not there. Sue's parents have asked her not to go to a friend's house unless parents will be home, or unless they know in advance and say it's OK.

▶ Barb thinks that her boyfriend's interest in her is cooling. She's noticed him looking at other girls more and sometimes openly flirting with them. She has decided to tell him she's willing to *go all the way*.

▶ Sharon feels empty and lonely, even when she is with the gang of kids she hangs out with at school. She feels self-conscious and awkward until she can drink a few beers. Lately the gang has been pairing off. The other girls tell her not to worry, that nothing really happens; you're just expected to give a little tongue and fool around. Sharon doesn't exactly know what that means, but she wants to be part of the group.

Summary

Close with a prayer asking for guidance in making decisions and for the courage to seek help and advice.

- How do you feel about what you've done in your action planning?
- What was helpful with this process? not helpful?
- Are there other places in your life where you might be able to use this process?

CLOSING WORSHIP (TOTAL GROUP)

(Allow 10 minutes.)

Use the following litany as you close the session. Ask the group to form a circle; pray for guidance in making decisions and for the courage to seek help and advice.

CELEBRATION OF OUR SEXUALITY

Leader: What do you have there?

Group: A sheet of paper. On it are printed two words.

Leader: What are the words?

Group: The word *God* and the word *sex*.

Leader: I have seen these words before, but I have never thought about God and sex together.

Group: God did a wondrous and curious thing in creating us. Sometimes it is hard to understand, the fact that God made us so different. Females and males act so differently, and all this is part of sex. From the beginning, sex has been a part of God's creation. God created us to be sexual persons, to be women and men.

Leader: So, this curious thing that God has done becomes a tremendous experience—my experience. In the Bible it says that when God had made male and female, man and woman, God said, "It is good."

Group: It is good—it's great! Our sexuality, our maleness and femaleness, is who we are. It's what we will be. We are turned loose to think, to talk, to decide.

Leader: It makes me feel strange to be so free. There is so much I want to know, and so much to know about. To think of God and sex at the same time, to say both in the same breath, takes your breath away!

Group: But it makes us feel good. We want to think, to talk, to know, to become the woman or man God created us to be. We want to use God's gift of sexuality to its fullest.

Leader: Praise God that I am a sexual being. Right?

Group: Right!

Leader: Thank God that I am free to discover, examine, and decide. Right?

Group: Right!

Leader: Amen.

ALL: And Amen!

God did a wondrous and curious thing in creating us.

5 Relationships

PURPOSE
To provide an opportunity for youth to explore their relationships as expressions of God's good gift of sexuality.

SCRIPTURE
Genesis 25–33; Genesis 37–50; Ruth 1–4; 1 Samuel 20; Mark 6:30-44; Luke 8:26-40; Luke 10:38-42; John 4:1-26; 1 Corinthians 13:4-7

Here's the Plan

Activities	Time	Preparation	Supplies
		Have CD or tape player playing.	CD or tape player
Relationships and Behaviors Story Board	45 minutes	Cover a wall with sheets of white paper that you can write on. List behaviors on pages 65–66 on index cards.	large pieces of paper, markers masking tape, index cards basket
Ideal Girl/Guy	30 minutes	Prepare four large sheets of paper, as directed on page 67.	marker, prepared papers
Bible Study on Relationships	10 minutes		Bible for each youth
Ideal Date (if you have more time)	10-15 minutes	Gather supplies.	large pieces of paper, tape, markers
Worship	5 minutes		

Relationships

PURPOSE: *To provide an opportunity for youth to explore their relationships as expressions of God's good gift of sexuality.*

FAITH FOCUS

Writers have referred to the teen years as the second birth. Children become adults before our eyes. Most of us received little help in developing mature relationships and avoiding some of the crushing experiences connected with break-ups and manipulations of mis-directed relationships. If any place models healthy relationships, it should be the church. Our wholeness and hope are based on our relationship with Jesus Christ. Many of the youth in our sexuality education sessions will have experienced the brokenness of divorce and the disappointment of parents whose covenant is expressed in abusive, degrading ways. Teens have lots of questions they need to ask and our responses can be sensitive to their current experiences and reflective of our commitment to relationships that support covenantal unity and grace.

COMMON GROUND

A solid relationship with God and others is crucial for any of us to successfully navigate through life. It is in our relationships, healthy or not, that we learn about ourselves, our feelings, our beliefs, attitudes, and values. We are each involved in many different kinds of relationships. We are sons and daughters, or mothers and fathers, or sisters and brothers, or friends, or husbands and wives, or boyfriend and girlfriend, lovers, partners . . . and the list goes on and on.

A meaningful relationship develops with time and is based on faith in each other, communication, acceptance, consideration, sharing a common goal, and enjoying time together. All adolescents take their relationships and

The leader should understand how males and females look at friendship differently.

friendships seriously, even though relationships and friendships fail quite often during this time of their lives.

Adolescence is a time for re-negotiation of beliefs, attitudes, and values. Understanding of friends, family, and dating is re-evaluated. When thinking and talking about sexuality and relationships, youth invariably want to know if there are appropriate behaviors.

It is important for adults to remember and acknowledge what occurs biologically during adolescence. Sex hormones begin production during puberty, and the body and mind start responding to sexual stimulation. All these processes are a natural part of God's creation.

It is important that youth know that being sexually active is not the only way to show that they care for someone in a relationship. Nor is being sexually active the only way to release their pent-up sexual feelings. They need to learn that there are many ways to be close to someone (holding hands, long talks, hugs, kisses, writing a letter, going to the movies, sharing dreams, thoughts, hopes, and concerns, attending a school activity or a church youth function, taking a walk) and that sharing affection does not necessarily include sexual behavior.

Sexuality isn't just a type of behavior or a physical act; it is also about self-esteem, feelings, attitudes, and how a person chooses to be in relationships. Sexuality is God's good gift. We need an understanding of the Word of God as a guide for building responsible, caring relationships.

AGE TO AGE

Males and females seek out and develop friendships and relationships differently. A very simple, generalizing statement about these differences might be as follows: Males tend to have friendships that are defined by activities: sports, church, clubs, and so forth. Guys talk less about themselves. "Doing" is the relationship. Female relationships are defined by "being." Females are more open and trusting and meet their emotional needs through sharing secrets and sharing stories. They don't have to do something or create something; they just enjoy dreaming, sharing, and talking together.

Stories of relationships can be found throughout the Bible.

There will be a vast difference in expressions about relationships between the middle-schoolers in the group and the older teens. Their expectations and maturity levels are sometimes miles apart. Keep this in mind, especially if you are unable to separate the age levels for the session.

GOD'S SAY

The Scripture highlighted in Session 5 of the student book, *Let's Decide,* is Romans 12:1-2. Please become familiar with these verses as well as the Scriptures given below. (Remember to read the Scriptures from the *Contemporary English Version.*)

Stories of relationships can be found throughout the Bible. In Genesis we find stories of the relationships that God developed with Adam and Eve. The covenant relationship of God and Israel is a never-ending story that is woven throughout the Old Testament. In the New Testament, Jesus' ministry is based on relationships with others. His relationship with the disciples; the relationships with Mary, Martha, and Lazarus; even the woman at the well, to name a few, are all examples of how important this image of relationship with others is. Jesus uses his relationships with friends and others in the Bible to teach the good news to all. These stories are relevant today because relationships affect many aspects of our lives.

Suggestions for further study:

Households of Faith

Jacob and Esau	Genesis 25–33
Joseph and his brothers	Genesis 37–50
Ruth's devotion	Ruth 1–4
Jonathan and David, best friends	1 Samuel 20

Jesus

demon-possessed man	Luke 8:26-40
Lazarus, Mary, and Martha	Luke 10:38-42
Samaritan woman	John 4:1-26

These are just a few examples of relationships in the Bible. The covenant that God makes with his people, the basis of all relationships, is the basis of the Old Testament, and Jesus and relationships are the strength of the New Testament.

STEP BY STEP

Before the session begins:
► Cover a wall with large sheets of paper in each family group setting.
► Have index cards with the following words written on them: Hugs, Kisses, Anger, Hate, Masturbation, Holding Hands, French Kissing, Fondling Each Other's Breasts, Playful Wrestling, Mutual Masturbation, Sexual Intercourse, Rape, Incest, Sexual Harassment, Date Rape, Marriage, Touching Each Other's Genitals, Love, Dating,

> The covenant that God makes with God's people is the basis of the Old Testament; Jesus and relationships are the strength of the New Testament.

Going Steady, Making Out, Fantasy, Getting Sexually Aroused, Petting, Breaking Up, Abstinence, Sexual Activity, Pregnancy. Place them into a bowl or some type of container so that the youth can draw out one at a time.

RELATIONSHIPS & BEHAVIORS STORY BOARD (FAMILY GROUPS)
(Allow 45 Minutes.)

Explain that the family group will create a story on the wall covered with large sheets of paper. Each person is to take blank index cards or strips of paper and a marker and write out different kinds of relationships that are part of his or her life (for example: brother, son, grandchild, boyfriend, aunt, uncle, parents, and so forth). Discuss these as you go along. Take turns placing these cards on the paper-covered wall. When these ideas have been exhausted, move on to the second part.

While they are posting these relationship cards, some major headings will become apparent, such as family, friends, dating relationships, marriage, God, and others. Have a volunteer write the headings that best fit your story so far. Your storyboard will now have headings and the different characters that belong under them across the wall.

Desired Result
To invite youth to consider that appropriate behaviors are connected to different kinds of relationships.

Bring out the container of index cards with different behaviors and orientations. Explain that on the cards are different behaviors, orientations, and words that they will select and place on the storyboard where they think they are appropriate. If the word is appropriate for more than one heading or relationship, be sure it is written wherever it applies. Let the group also come up with their own terms. They may realize in their process that they want a heading called "never appropriate," or something like that. Remember the idea is to create your story about different kinds of relationships and different behaviors that go along with those relationships. The participants will think differently on what and when something is appropriate. There should be enough space on your storyboard wall to include these differences.

Note: It may help to remember to define things (for example, ages of the different characters, or words that have more than one meaning).

Open-ended questions such as these can help keep the story and the discussion going:

▶ Tell us more about why you placed that card where it is.
▶ What do you think would be a more appropriate behavior?
▶ What other things would you add?

IDEAL GIRL/GUY (TOTAL GROUP)
(Allow 30 minutes.)

▶ **Before the session,** prepare four large sheets of paper with the following headings:

Girls: 1. What we think boys look for in the ideal girl.
      2. What we look for in the ideal boy. (Keep this sheet covered until you are finished with the first one.)

Boys: 1. What we think girls look for in the ideal boy.
      2. What we look for in the ideal girl. (Keep this sheet covered until you are finished with the first one.)

Explain that all the girls will meet together and all the guys will meet together. They will have ten minutes to describe the ideal person of the opposite sex. Have the two groups separate and move to different rooms where they cannot hear one another. Each group should have the two appropriate sheets of paper for their group. (**Girls:** What we think guys look for in the ideal girl. What we look for in the ideal guy. **Guys:** What we think girls look for in the ideal guy. What we look for in the ideal girl.)

Bring the group back together after ten minutes. Create a fishbowl circle with the guys sitting inside the girls' circle. The girls are instructed to listen and make no comments while the guys read off what they look for in an ideal girl. When they are finished, the girls will read off their list of what they think guys look for in an ideal girl. Tell the guys to listen and make no comments until the girls are finished. Then reverse the circles and have the girls read their second sheet while the guys listen. Finally, the girls are to listen while the guys tell what they think girls look for in the ideal boy.

Then ask:
▶ Do you hear any similarities?
▶ Do you now have any comments or questions?
▶ What can you say about how we see sexuality differently as male or as female?
▶ How did this activity make you feel?
▶ Were you surprised by anything the other group wrote?

End with: "Both of the lists included lots of different ideas about what makes an ideal person. What is attractive to one person will not necessarily be so for another. It is important to remember that ideals are dreams and fantasy, and that each of us is a real person with feelings. What kinds of words would God use to describe relationships? (love, respect, kindness, understanding, patience) God's words to us would be, "Think on these things."

The youth will have ten minutes to describe the ideal person of the opposite sex.

Desired Result
To have fun and learn to the unique ways each gender views the other

BIBLE STUDY ON RELATIONSHIPS (FAMILY GROUPS)
(Allow 10 minutes.)

Be sure that youth have their Bibles with them. Ask for volunteers to read aloud the following passages. As the passages are read, use the questions for discussion starters.

> "Some friends don't help, but a true friend is closer than your own family" (Proverbs 18:24).

What does this say to you about friends, and about being a friend?

> "A friend is always a friend, and relatives are born to share our troubles" (Proverbs 17:17).

What do you think this means about our families?

> "Don't make friends with anyone who has a bad temper. You might turn out like them and get caught in a trap" (Proverbs 22:24-25).

Why is it so important to choose your friends wisely? What happens to us when we are asked to do something that we know is wrong?

> "Now I tell you to love each other, as I have loved you. The greatest way to show love for friends is to die for them. And you are my friends, if you obey me. Servants don't know what their master is doing, and so I don't speak to you as my servants. I speak to you as my friends, and I have told you everything that my Father has told me. You did not choose me. I chose you and sent you out to produce fruit, the kind of fruit that will last. Then my Father will give you whatever you ask for in my name. So I command you to love each other" (John 15:12-17).

What does Jesus ask in return for his friendship? How does love relate to this friendship?

What does this say to you about friends, and about being a friend?

IF YOU HAVE MORE TIME

IDEAL DATE (FAMILY GROUPS)
(Allow 10–15 minutes.)

Consider this suggestion if you have more time. Have the family group decide what to do on a date with $10, $50, or $100, using the decision-making skills they have practiced. Have someone write on large sheets of paper the plans for the date.

Ask: "What does everyone think of these ideas? Does this date sound fun to you? Why or why not?"

With your senior-high age group, ask:
"Who usually pays for the date?"
"Who asks whom out? Boys, would you go on a date if a girl asked you out and paid for everything?"
"Girls, how would you feel about going Dutch to the Junior/Senior prom?"

Closing Worship
(*Allow 5 minutes.*)
Have the group form a circle and share with one another a positive statement about the person standing to their right. Share any prayer concerns or joys, and close with a group prayer.

Share any prayer concerns or joys, and close with a group prayer.

COMMON GROUND ADDENDUM

A tremendous amount of information is available today about rape, molestation, harassment, sexual and physical abuse, and date rape. Consider having another session to discuss these issues and their ramifications in a youth's life. In many areas of the country there are specially-trained people who will come and talk to your group. If you feel uncomfortable leading such a discussion, a guest speaker would be a good idea. Look for a speaker or information at a rape crisis center, the police department, the YWCA, or the Department of Human Services. Many phone books will also list valuable resources.

▶ **Before the session** rent a copy of *Disclosures* with Demi Moore and Michael Douglas, and select several vignettes showing how Michael experiences harassment. Prepare several questions for discussion. Most people feel that only women are discriminated against, so this activity will add to the discussion that anyone can be a victim of sexual harassment. This movie is rated "R," so remember this as you choose the vignettes. (**NOTE: A license is needed from the Motion Picture Licensing Board for showing copyrighted videos. Call 800-515-8855.**)

News articles about these issues are good discussion starters. Prepare several open-ended questions to begin the discussion. You can also inquire about police procedures on specific topics in your area and find out your local school policies concerning sexual harassment.

In the age of instant gratification and media saturation, adolescents see, and sometimes develop, defective and dysfunctional attitudes about who they are as God's good gifts and how to relate to others. As discussed in session 1, multimedia reflects unrealistic and distorted images of who adolescents are and how friendships and relationships develop. The perceived goal, many times, is instant personal satisfaction. With this skewed attitude, many adolescents are involved in unhealthy relationships, which can lead to date rape, molestation or sexual abuse, and sexual harassment.

Youth need to know there are people they can turn to in such cases. Attending a group such as this might bring up these sensitive issues. Be prepared to deal with these issues in a healthy and caring way. These youth may feel it was their fault. Their self-esteem may be non-existent. They can be pushing their feelings far inside themselves, hoping to forget the experience, but causing their behavior to change drastically (usually for the worse). Be aware of warning signs of adolescents who might be in abusive situations.

Be aware of warning signs of adolescents who might be in abusive situations.

Adolescents need to be told how to recognize manipulation and abuse and reassured that this type of relationship is wrong. One person does not have the right to control another through threats of blackmail, shame, or guilt. Young people need to know that this manipulation is wrong, and that there are safe adults who will help them, and be with them throughout the ordeal.

In *Reducing the Risk of Child Sexual Abuse in Your Church* by Richard R. Hammar, Steven W. Klipowowicz, and James F. Cobble, Jr. (Christian Ministry Resources, Matthews, CA, 1993), the following signals that abuse might have happened, or is now happening, are given:

SYMPTOMS OF MOLESTATION

Physical signs may include
► lacerations and bruises
► nightmares
► irritation, pain, or injury to the genital area
► difficulty with urination
► difficulty when sitting
► torn or bloody underclothing
► STIs

Behavioral signs may include
► anxiety when approaching a certain area
► nervous or hostile behavior towards adults
► sexual self-consciousness
► "acting out" of sexual behavior
► withdrawal from church activities and friends

Let's Be Real: Honest Discussions About Faith and Sexuality

Also listen for verbal signs from youth. If they don't want to be alone with a particular person, seem unreasonable in their dislike of a person, or say that they don't like what he or she does, consider this a warning and encourage them to tell you why they feel this way.

Signs of possible abuse or neglect

- self-destruction and destructive behavior
- fractures, lacerations, bruises that cannot be explained or explanations that are improbable, given a child's development stage
- depression, passiveness
- hyperactive/disruptive behavior
- sexualized behavior or precocious knowledge, pseudo-maturity
- running away, promiscuous behavior
- alcohol or drug abuse, other self-destructive behavior such as eating disorders
- poor peer relationships
- self-mutilation
- problems with authority
- somatic complaints, including pain and irritation of genitals
- STIs
- pregnancy in young adolescents
- frequent unexplained sore throats, yeast infections, urinary infections
- avoidance of undressing or wearing extra layers of clothes
- sudden avoidance of certain familiar adults or places
- decline in school performance
- sleep disturbances

Dating Violence

Dating violence crosses all cultural and socio-economic barriers. It is found in large metropolitan areas as well as the rural areas. No county, town, or community is exempt from this problem today. Dating violence is described as emotional abuse, physical abuse, or sexual abuse in a dating or acquaintance relationship.

Acquaintance rape is commonly called date rape. Date rape is a misleading term, which describes a serious crime that is misunderstood and under reported. Rape is a felony sexual assault that leaves the victim injured and traumatized. Victims of rape, especially rape committed by an acquaintance, often feel a sense of responsibility for the attacks and don't report the crime to police. Acquaintance rape is fostered by the common sex role stereotype that men should be competitive and aggressive, while women should be yielding and passive. Experts advise women to be open and assertive from the start of a relationship, to prevent any misunderstanding with their date.

Our society is obsessed with sexual violence in the media.

Why does date rape happen?

1. Our society is obsessed with sexual violence in the media.

2. Pornography reinforces the myth that women want sex even when they say no, or if it is painful.

3. Men are brought up to be aggressive and masculine. This includes pressure to score from peers and to pursue fun. Women are brought up to be feminine. They want romance, to find Mr. Right.

Some Date Rape Facts to Ponder

4. Sexual violence is also a product of society's strong endorsement of drinking alcohol. An incredible seventy-five percent of all date rapes involve alcohol or drug abuse. Think of the beer commercials you have seen; think of how many are targeting teen guys.

5. In the Christian community, date rape sadly occurs because of all of the reasons above. In an ongoing survey of evangelical teens between the ages of thirteen and eighteen, Macro Computer Solutions (MCS) found that seventy-five percent of them have seen the movie *Basic Instinct*! There is something wrong with this picture.

Some Date Rape Facts to Ponder

Facts
- Only one percent of all date rapes are ever reported.
- Fifty-seven percent of all rapes happen on dates.
- One out of three women will be sexually assaulted in her lifetime.
- Seventy-five percent of all date rapes involve alcohol or drug abuse.
- Numerous studies conclude that pornography desensitizes men to sexual violence and rape.
- These studies also conclude that pornography has an addictive quality and that men who become addicted have a need for more graphic and violent pornography.
- Most date rape victims believe that the crime was somehow their fault, that they provoked it by something they said or didn't say, or by the way they dressed.

Date rape is never the victim's fault. Victims may find themselves in dangerous situations because of poor judgment; but no one has the right to violate your body, even if he or she is aroused.

Taking sex from someone does not lead to intimacy, and it is not an achievement to boast about with your friends, or to be proud of.

Profile of a Date Rapist

Psychologists have identified some key personality traits of potential rapists:

▶ They begin sexual intercourse at an earlier age.

▶ They tend to talk about sex a great deal, including sexual positions, sexual body parts, and so forth.

▶ They feel that sex is an achievement; it makes them feel important, powerful, and in control.

▶ They are con artists who use only a moderate amount of force.

▶ They generally have poor communication skills with the opposite sex.

▶ They are almost always into pornography, whether it's magazines, videos, music, or all of the above.

Internet sites on date rape:

▶ http://foghorn.usfca.edu.archives/spring96/fl5/features/facts.html
▶ http://www.discribe.ca/fsacc/ar&dr.hte
▶ http://www.mcs-special-support.com/abuse/sexual_and_assault/ rape.html
▶ http://santamonicpd.org/text/tdate.htm
▶ http://www.hartinc.com/siv/rape.htm (This a review of a video on date rape.)

The New Date Rape Drug of Choice

Rohypnol, or **roofies** as it is being called on the street, is the new date rape drug of choice. It is also called **ruffies, roche, R-2, rib,** and **rope.**

Rohypnol is a brand name of **flunitrazepam (a benzodiazepine)**, a very potent tranquilizer similar in nature to Valium (diazepam), but many times stronger. The drug produces a sedative effect, amnesia, muscle relaxation, and a slowing of psycho-motor responses. Sedation occurs twenty to thirty minutes after administration and lasts for several hours.

Other drugs, including **gamma hydroxbutyrate (GHB)**, a liquid made of ingredients available in health food stores, are being used in bars, clubs, and at parties as a cheap way of getting high; and they are also used as date rape drugs.

These drugs can have deadly consequences. GHB, which can depress breathing, can cut oxygen to the brain. Rohypnol comes from the same family as Zanax, Valium, Librium, and Halcion. It works by interfering with chemical activity in the brain. It causes intoxication with slurred speech, difficulty in walking, and impaired judgment. In combination with alcohol, Rohypnol can kill. It is tasteless, colorless and odorless, and it dissolves quickly in drinks. It causes amnesia and loss of inhibitions for up to twelve hours.

The following publications contain valuable information on rape and dating.

Check out these other good resources:

Unmasking Sexual Con Games (Boys Town Press, Boys Town, Nebraska, 1993).

An excellent resource for parents and teens is *What Parents Need to Know About Dating Violence* by Barrie Levy and Patricia Occhiuzzo Giggans (Seal Press, 1995).

In Love and in Danger: A Teen's Guide to Breaking Free of Abusive Relationships, by Barrie Levy (Seal Press, 1993).

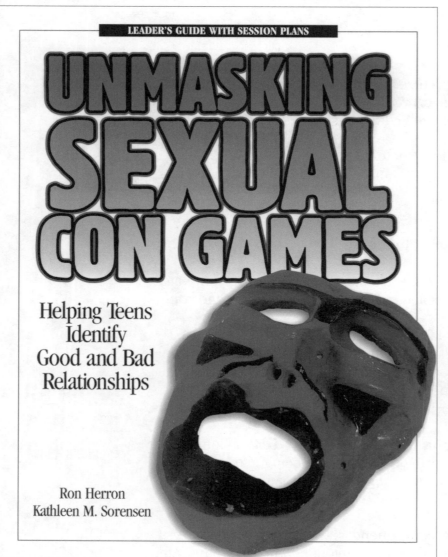

LEADER'S GUIDE WITH SESSION PLANS

UNMASKING SEXUAL CON GAMES

Helping Teens Identify Good and Bad Relationships

Ron Herron
Kathleen M. Sorensen

For further study with your youth group, use the charts and stories in the book *In Love and in Danger* as a starting point for an honest and open discussion about date rape and dating violence. If you decide to have an extra session, below are some suggestions that could be worked into this session on violence, abuse, and rape.

Bible Study
The Bible has very strict rules about rape and incest. Have a youth read about marriage violations in Deuteronomy 22:13-30. Then ask:

"Why do you think the penalty for improper sexual and social behavior was so harsh?"

"Have God's restrictions on sexual behavior changed?"

"Does our society have laws that reflect the rules in this passage?"

Read aloud Genesis 34:1-31; and then read the excerpt below from *The Storyteller's Companion to the Bible,* Volume 4, edited by Michael E. Williams (Abingdon Press, 1993; pages 52–54).

Retelling the Story

She hated it when her brothers talked about her in her presence, because they always treated her as if she were in a coma, or worse, a piece of dead wood. They never talked to her, asked her feelings, her opinion. They talked about her as if she were one of their donkeys or camels, and she knew that though they spoke of their love for her as their sister, she was considered little more than livestock.

Such was the situation for a woman of the Middle East. Each morning men thanked God they had not been born female. Here sons were called "ben," or "son of," followed by their father's name, though it was their mothers who bled and screamed, nursed and wept over them. Here fathers' names were changed when a son arrived and were called "abu," or "father of," their eldest son. Daughters were considered a liability.

For all the differences among the many tribes that fought and killed each other over these hillsides and grazing lands, they were bound together by at least two firmly held convictions. These were a mutual distrust for anyone who was different and the idea that women were the property of men.

Dinah's current predicament was the perfect example. Shechem had raped her; there was no other word for it. It was brutal and humiliating. She had done nothing to provoke this young stranger's attention. Even so, throughout the attack he acted as if she had been the instigator. "You wanted it," he kept repeating. All she really wanted was for this living nightmare to be over. Even after the initial physical pain began to subside, waves of nausea swept over her, and what she wished more than anything in the world was that he had killed her instead.

Now her brothers were shouting in angry voices about how *their* honor had been violated, and their eyes burned with revenge for what had happened to *them*. "Stop it!" she heard her own voice repeating more loudly each time she

Did God hear her, or was God just a larger version of her brothers, railing against offenses, against some divine code of honor while all the time ignoring her?

said it. But her brothers gave no indication that they heard her. Were her screams on the inside only, so that her pain was unheard by any human ear other than her own? Did God hear her, or was her God just a larger version of her brothers, railing against offenses, against some divine code of honor while all the time ignoring her hurt?

Now the voices around her were whispers, as if their shouts for revenge had transformed to plotting it. She heard the words "foreskins," "the sign of Abraham," and "marriage." Surely they did not intend to give her in marriage to her rapist, even if he did agree to be circumcised! Not even her brothers could be that insensitive to her plight. Would they sacrifice their sister when Abraham had not sacrificed his son? She wept and prayed for a lamb in the thicket, for some way out of such an unimaginable fate. Could the same God the men invoked in their battles against their enemies also be called to the side of a woman violated by her enemy, ignored by her family, and traded like a donkey?

Today, many people are oppressed throughout the world. Discuss how this kind of story still happens today.

You might want to read the materials on sexual harassment in the youth resource, pages 30–34, and the resources listed on page 118.

CLOSING WORSHIP

Closing worship for this extra session might focus on 1 Corinthians 13, often called the "love chapter." This passage follows a discussion of spiritual gifts and what it means to be a part of the "body of Christ." In Chapter 13, Paul shares the significance of love as the vital element for people to be in relationship. Verses 4-7 focus on some very practical aspects of love in human relations.

Give each youth a copy of 1 Corinthians 13:4-7. Read the passage together. Comment on the Scripture based on the information given above. Considering the seriousness of the topics you have just covered, reinforce the idea that God's way is love.

Explain that you will all read the passage together again. This time, however, each person will insert his or her name in place of the word *love*.

Follow this with a prayer that allows the participants to ask questions pertaining to the passage: "God, as we come to you in prayer now, we seek to understand what it means to relate to others. We have read

Scripture about what it means to be loving in our relationships. Help us sort those words out so we can understand what they mean for us.

God, am I patient?
Am I kind?
When am I envious, boastful, or arrogant?
Am I rude?
Do I insist on my own way?
When am I irritable or resentful?
Do I rejoice in wrongdoing, or the truth?

God, help me to bear all things, believe all things, be hopeful, and endure when I need to. In Christ's name. Amen."

God, help me to bear all things, believe all things, be hopeful, and endure when I need to. Amen.

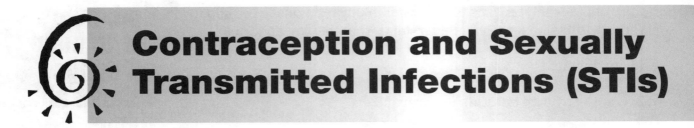

Contraception and Sexually Transmitted Infections (STIs)

PURPOSE
To present abstinence as the most viable, desirable, and faithful choice, yet still educate youth about contraceptive alternatives, sexually transmitted infections, and the risks associated with both.

SCRIPTURE
Romans 12:1-2

Here's the Plan

Activities	Time	Preparation	Supplies
I Choose (Senior High)	30 minutes	Make "I Choose" cards.	index cards, large sheets of paper, masking tape, markers
Contraceptive Picture Charades (Senior High)	30 minutes	Photocopy **selected** contraceptive cards from pages 90–91, and cut them apart.	chalk/dry erase board, chalk or markers
STI Case Study (Senior High)	20 minutes	Photocopy STI sheets, page 92.	photocopies
What They Know (Middle School)	10 minutes	Prepare three sheets of paper labeled Abstinence, Contraceptives, and Sexually Transmitted Infections.	tape, pencils or markers
Contraceptive Methods (Middle School)	20 minutes	Write contraceptive methods and percentage of effectiveness (pages 90–91) on index cards.	index cards
An Infectious Game (Middle School)	30 minutes	Gather colored cards for game.	colored index cards
What Can Happen? (Middle School)	20 minutes		
Commitment Service (Total Group)	25 minutes	Purchase wrapped chocolate candies for the group. Obtain copy of your denomination's marriage ceremony. Make copies of "Promise Card" on page 93.	candy, marriage ceremony, photocopies

Let's Be Real: Honest Discussions About Faith and Sexuality

Contraception and Sexually Transmitted Infections (STIs)

PURPOSE: *To present abstinence as the most viable, desirable, and faithful choice, yet still educate youth about contraceptive alternatives, sexually transmitted infections, and the risks associated with both.*

Note: This session is designed to last at least two hours. Even more time is required if you end this study with a special celebration.

FAITH FOCUS

We can't help our youth understand their sexuality without confronting the reality of life-threatening STIs. We can't afford to depend on youth to raise the issue. We can be clear that the best way to prevent becoming infected is by not having any type of sexual intercourse. The reality is that many teens are not waiting till marriage to have intercourse. Therefore, we must help youth protect themselves if this is the decision they make. Although it's difficult and demanding, we must learn how to help teens learn to use protective devices and techniques that will avoid unwanted pregnancy and disease. This includes addressing drug and alcohol use that impairs judgment. Giving good information does not imply giving permission.

COMMON GROUND

These are possibly the most controversial topics of the curriculum. There are several schools of thought about how these topics should be handled, or if the church should even deal with them. There are feelings that if the church doesn't acknowledge birth control, its youth will not get pregnant. If we do not deal with STIs, we will not have youth getting infected. For us to ignore the information that youth who are active in church might also be as sexually active as the rest of the youth population would be folly.

Recent information from the National Center for Health Statistics indicates that sexual activity among teens is now declining for the first time since the federal government began keeping records. This information, coupled with the decline of the teen birth rate since 1991,

Young people want and need accurate and comprehensive information from the church to help them make the transition to adulthood.

A teen must think about abstinence as a mature, practical, viable, and faithful choice.

gives hope that youth are making better decisions. These decisions include choosing to abstain from sexual intercourse, delaying sexual activity, and becoming more informed about the use of protection when choosing to be sexually active.

At a time when one in four sexually active teens is expected to contract a sexually transmitted infection, it is important to continue to provide youth with information that will enable them to make knowledgeable decisions. In the youth resource, *Let's Decide: Faith and My Sexuality,* and the following session material, factual information to assist teens who might be considering sexual activity is presented.

Abstinence is the ideal for people of faith who are single. Infections and pregnancies are almost obliterated if there is no sexual intercourse. The question is, how do you help youth choose abstinence, and how do they interpret what that means for them? Abstinence can mean anything, from no physical touching to every expression of intimacy except sexual intercourse. Helping youth sort out all of the messages about abstinence can be a challenge. Believing God calls us to a relationship of love and commitment in marriage can help us guide our youth in this area.

A teen must think about abstinence as a mature, practical, viable, and faithful choice. Not considering abstinence or making a conscious decision to abstain can actually be more dangerous than making an informed choice to be sexually active. When a teen says, "I'm waiting to be sexually active," but has not thought through what that means, he or she is at higher risk of pregnancy and infection because of not considering any forms of protection. The teen may actually be more likely to be involved in unprotected, unplanned, and therefore dangerous sexual activity.

When youth choose abstinence, they need to understand their reasons for their choice. Do they believe God's plan is for our sexuality to be fully expressed as a part of our commitment to another in marriage? Have they chosen this because they are not ready for intimacy? Are they abstaining because they have not met the right person? Are they concerned about infection and pregnancy? Reasons could include any of these, others not listed, or a combination.

For youth to live out their choice of abstinence it is helpful for them to know their reasons and be able to articulate their reasons to others. In order to help youth choose abstinence, we need to help them with reasons to support their choice. Most importantly, any person with whom the youth is in a relationship needs to be aware of the decision and willing to support him or her in that decision. The idea that "everybody's doing it" is not accurate—at least fifty percent of teens have chosen not to have intercourse by the time they are seventeen years old.

AGE TO AGE

"It won't happen to me!"
"If it happens, we can take care of it!"
"Everybody's gotta die sometime; I might as well enjoy myself!"

These might be statements youth make about the consequences of sexual activity. Some teens believe that they can do anything and they will survive. Others believe that no matter what happens, they, their parents, or someone else will be able to make it OK again. There is also a group who believes in a fatalistic view of life. This group feels little hope; therefore, they see no reason to be concerned about what COULD happen. Other youth are realistic, have refined their values, have a sense of self-worth, and derive meaning for life from a genuine faith.

As you look at the issues in this session, remember that you will need to respond with hope, grace, and love to all the youth involved.

As youth think about decisions concerning their bodies and God's gift of sexuality, this message of purity is vital!

GOD'S SAY

The Scripture in this session is a part of Paul's letter to the Romans. This letter has the purpose of helping the Christians in Rome understand how God can make acceptable each person who has sinned. Romans 12:1-2 begins a section on wholesome and Christian living. It is the preface to a section offering practical advice on how to live as a committed Christian in an un-Christian world. (Sound appropriate?) Obviously, priority is given to the importance of the body. As youth think about decisions concerning their bodies and God's gift of sexuality, this message of purity is vital! We not only make decisions based on what could happen (consequences), but also consider what is right and holy. At this point, we move to a higher plane of understanding. Getting by is not enough. Paul calls us to offer God our best self as "a living sacrifice, pure and pleasing."

STEP BY STEP

Supplies

- ▶ cards prepared for the "I Choose" exercise (below) for senior high youth
- ▶ large sheets of paper
- ▶ markers
- ▶ cards from "Contraceptives Chart"
- ▶ STI Information Sheet
- ▶ color cards for the "Infectious Game" (page 87)
- ▶ boom box
- ▶ lively music
- ▶ hugs candy (enough for each participant)
- ▶ "Promise Card" (page 93)
- ▶ provisions for celebration

Schedule

Senior High	Middle School
▶ 30 minutes—I Choose	10 minutes—What They Know
▶ 30 minutes—Contraceptive Picture Charades	20 minutes—Birth Control Methods
▶ 20 minutes—Case Study	30 minutes—An Infectious Game
	20 minutes—What Can Happen?

Total Group

- ▶ 25 minutes—Worship Celebration

I CHOOSE (SENIOR HIGH)
(Allow 30 minutes.)

This exercise is designed to help youth understand their freedom to choose when it comes to serious, sexual activity and consequences. It should take place in Family Groups. Give each youth a card with a statement similar to one of the following printed on it (each person should have a card):

I CHOOSE...to go fishing.
I CHOOSE...to make friends with persons who are different from me.
I CHOOSE...to cut my hair.
I CHOOSE...to be funny.

This exercise is designed to help youth understand their freedom to choose when it comes to serious sexual activity and the consequences.

Desired Result
To support youth as they claim their freedom and responsibility in making faithful choices.

I CHOOSE...making money over having fun.
I CHOOSE...life in a cabin by myself.
I CHOOSE...to ride a bike rather than drive a car.

When all of the participants have a card, ask them to find a partner. Have the partners tell each other whether they would make the choice on the card. Ask them how their response would change if someone else were doing the choosing, such as a parent, a friend, or a close relative. (How does a parent choosing to have your hair cut change your feelings about your hair being cut?)

Ask the youth to tell you the situations in which they make their own decisions. Make a list of these on a large sheet of paper. Make another list with situations where youth are not allowed to make their own decisions. (You will probably end up with some items on both sheets because different youth have different freedoms in decision-making.)

Choice Discussion

This discussion should touch on issues of decision-making, protection, and abstinence raised in earlier sessions. You are helping youth think about who is really making decisions. They will need to wrestle with the question of decision-making by default—when is not making a decision actually making a decision? Discuss the consequences as they relate to the topics presented in the questions below.

> **Ask:**
> ▶ How does not making decisions apply to your sexuality?
> ▶ Do we choose to become pregnant or to get someone pregnant?
> ▶ What is the decision-making process?
> ▶ Do we choose to infect someone or to be infected by STIs?
> ▶ What decisions lead to or prevent infection?
> ▶ Can we choose not to be sexually active?
> ▶ What does that mean for us socially? spiritually? physically?

CONTRACEPTIVE PICTURE CHARADES (SENIOR HIGH)
(*Allow 30 minutes.*)

Before the session, cut out selected cards from the "Contraceptive Chart," pages 90–91. Each contraceptive method is listed with:

▶ information regarding effectiveness (in percentage rates of births per 100 women annually);
▶ source (whether prescribed, over the counter, and so forth);
▶ method of use, possible side effects, and any benefits for protection against STIs.

(Birth control methods are also listed in the *Let's Decide,* pages 36–38.)

This discussion should touch on issues of decision-making, protection, and abstinence from earlier sessions.

Remind the youth that abstinence is the only 100-percent-effective birth control method.

Give the cards to the teens. (Some teens may have more than one card, depending on the size of the group.) Ask for a volunteer to draw this or her method on a large sheet of paper or on a chalkboard. Let others guess until the method has been identified. When the method is identified, ask the teen to share other information from the card. (An example or picture of the method is helpful so that the youth can actually see it.)

Remind the youth that abstinence is the only 100-percent-effective birth control method.

STI Case Study (Senior High)
(Allow 20 minutes.)

Share the following case study with your family group:

Josh and Christie have had an ongoing relationship for over six months. They had not moved beyond French kissing and some light touching until about a month ago. One night, they were in the basement of Jim's house watching a movie, when no one else was at home. The movie was romantic, and things soon got heavy. Before Josh and Christie knew what had happened, they had moved from touching to sexual intercourse. It was a surprise for both of them, and they had not made any decisions about protection.

Desired Result
To give youth an opportunity to practice decision-making in a case study.

Because what happened was unexpected, things cooled for a while in the relationship. Then a couple of days ago, Christie found Josh at school and said that they needed to talk. When they were alone, Christie started to cry. Josh didn't know what was wrong, so he put his arm around her and asked.

"I don't know how to start," she said between sobs.

Josh suggested that she just say whatever she needed to say. So, slowly, Christie got the story out. It seems that before Josh, there had been another guy. They had also gone all the way—that's why she broke up with him. She had decided she wasn't ready for that kind of intimacy. She had just found out that she has an STI. She thinks that she must have gotten it from the first guy. She is afraid that she may have given it to Josh.

Discuss the following questions:

▶ How would you react if you were Josh?
▶ What if Josh had no symptoms?
▶ Where could both Josh and Christie go for help?
▶ What are some infections and symptoms they both could have?
▶ Which STIs are not treatable?
▶ What is the only sure way to avoid STIs, including HIV?

Be sure that the discussion covers the essentials from the "STI Information Sheet," page 92.

Let's Be Real: Honest Discussions About Faith and Sexuality

WHAT THEY KNOW (MIDDLE SCHOOL)
(Allow 10 minutes.)

Before the youth arrive, put three large sheets of paper on the wall. Write one of the following words on each:

Abstinence
Contraceptives
Sexually Transmitted Infections

Ask the youth to put any words that come to mind on the sheets. You should get a list that at least has some words and phrases describing what each word means or methods and types for the **Contraceptives** and the **STIs.** Say that this is a way to clarify what we already know about these topics so that we can learn more.

In a total group presentation, tell the following information:

Abstinence is the ideal for single persons. The risk of infection or pregnancy is almost obliterated if there is no sexual intercourse. The questions to think about are, "How do I choose abstinence?" and "How do I interpret what that means?"

For different people, abstinence means different things. *Abstinence* can mean anything from no physical touching or expression of intimacy, to some degree of touching or expression of intimacy; **but it always means "no sexual intercourse."** Believing that God calls us to a relationship of love and commitment in marriage can help guide us in this area.

Many Christians make this decision because they believe that God intended sexual intercourse to be a way that a man and woman come together as one—both physically and spiritually.

"That's why a man will leave his own father and mother. He marries a woman, and the two of them become like one person" (Genesis 2:24). (Share other information from the "Common Ground" section as you choose.)

Contraceptives, or birth control methods, are used to stop a person who is sexually active from getting pregnant, or from getting someone pregnant. Different methods have different rates of effectiveness. (Distribute the "Contraceptives Chart," pages 90–91.) There are two major forms of birth control or contraception.

Abstinence can mean anything from no physical touching or expression of intimacy, to some degree of touching or expression of intimacy; but it always means "no sexual intercourse."

One form is called a **barrier method.** These methods are designed to keep the sperm and the egg from uniting. If the sperm and egg do not unite, there can be no fertilization, and therefore no pregnancy.

The other form of birth control is **chemical.** Chemical methods change the chemical makeup of the woman to keep an egg from being released each month, or to keep the fertilized egg from attaching to the uterus. In addition, there are several other forms of birth control we will look at together. Persons not engaging in sexual intercourse are not at risk for pregnancy.

There are many myths about transmission of STIs.

STIs (Sexually Transmitted Infections) are just that—infections that can be transmitted from one sexual partner to another during oral, vaginal, or anal intercourse. (Hand out the "STI Information Sheet," page 92.) While there are ways that STIs can be transmitted without intercourse (for example, a person can be at risk for HIV when engaging in intravenous drug use and other activities where body fluids are exchanged), generally persons not engaging in intercourse are not at risk for contracting or passing an STI.

There are many myths about transmission of STIs.

Generally speaking, you are not at risk from activities like touching doorknobs, using public toilets, or casual interaction with an HIV-positive person. You might ask if youth have heard of any other risky activities.

CONTRACEPTIVE METHODS (MIDDLE SCHOOL)
   (*Allow 20 minutes.*)

Hand out cards with one type of contraceptive method listed on each, along with information concerning effectiveness (in percentage rates of births per 100 women annually), source (whether prescribed, over the counter, and so on), method of use, possible side effects, and any benefits for protection against STIs. The information for this is available in the Contraceptives Chart on pages 90–91, and some of it is also given on pages 36–38 in the student resource. Have three large sheets of paper on the wall, labeled Barrier, Chemical, and Other. Ask those with cards to read their card to the group, and then, with the help of the group, decide where it belongs. As the method information is shared with the group, add other information including a sample or picture and information concerning use and abuse of the product. Ask if there are additional questions about contraception. Remind the youth that there is a section on the topic in their student book if they need information later. Be sure that abstinence is included in this discussion of contraception as the only "for sure" way to avoid pregnancy and STIs. Abstinence is also considered the appropriate choice for unmarried people by most Christian groups.

AN INFECTIOUS GAME (MIDDLE SCHOOL)

(Allow 30 minutes.)

For this game, each teen will receive a colored card (construction paper, index card, and so forth). You will want to give one person a color that only he or she receives. One-tenth of the youth (10 percent) of the group will receive a different color. Give half the group (50 percent) the next color card. The remainder of the youth will receive a different color card.

Have the group move around as you play music. When the music stops, have them find a partner and sign each other's card. Continue this process four more times, and then ask the youth to sit down.

Ask the person with the single card to stand. Ask those who signed that card to stand. Have everyone else whose card has the signature of a person who is standing to also stand.

Ask anyone who has these persons' signatures to stand. (Your whole group should be standing at this point.) Have those with the color given to half the group sit down.

Say: "These people represent the 50 percent of youth who have chosen to be abstinent. They are not at risk of contracting an STI."

Have those with the 10 percent card color sit down.

Say: "These people represent the percentage of sexually active people who use latex condoms. They are unlikely to contract an STI if the condom is used correctly."

The other youth are at risk of getting one of a number of STIs. Remind the group that half of them were not at risk because they had chosen abstinence.

Ask for feelings about the game. Have the group look at the "STI Information Sheet" and ask if there are any questions. You may want to go over the general section on symptoms and treatments. Remind the youth that there is virtually no risk of contracting an STI if you practice abstinence, do not share intravenous needles, or participate in any other activity that exchanges body fluids.

Remind the youth that there is virtually no risk of contracting an STI if you practice abstinence, do not share intravenous needles, or participate in any other activity that exchanges body fluids.

WHAT CAN HAPPEN? (MIDDLE SCHOOL/FAMILY GROUPS)
(*Allow 20 minutes.*)

Read the following scenario to your family group:

Jeff and Jean have known each other "forever." They are both in eighth grade and have been together since their parents took them to the park in their strollers. Recently, they have started talking about the things that are happening to their bodies and wondering what it would be like to "have sex" like they see on TV and in the movies.

Ask your group about the possible outcomes of this conversation and the consequences involved.

Possible outcomes and consequences (do not reveal these unless the youth do not come up with them):

Jeff and Jean choose not to have sexual intercourse.
> They decide their friendship is too important.
> No STI or pregnancy could happen.
> They feel good because they have made the decision that they believe God wants for them.
> They don't feel guilty.

Jeff and Jean have sexual intercourse.
> They worry about the possibility of Jean's getting pregnant.
> Though they know it's not supposed to happen, they worry about STIs.
> They feel guilty, because they know that their decision doesn't fit with their faith or their family's values.

Ask: Which decision is a healthier decision for Jeff and Jean? Why?

COMMITMENT SERVICE (TOTAL GROUP)
(*Allow 25 minutes.*)

Give each person a wrapped chocolate candy as he or she enters the room for worship. Ask the participants to hold on to their candy until you give the other directions.

Begin the worship period with this statement or something similar:

"During this experience, we have talked about who we are—people created as sexual beings by God. We've looked at the media, how our bodies look and work, decision-making, relationships, and information about contraceptives and infections. We've gotten to know one another and to explore these issues together. Now it's time for us to think about what all of this means for us as people of God."

Now it's time for us to think about what all of this means for us as people of God.

Say: "Everyone eat your candy. [Have the participants pass the wrappers to a central location and have someone ready to collect them.) Who would like another?" (Many will raise their hand.)

"Who thinks that they could eat ten right now?" (Some will still raise their hands.)

"Who thinks that they could eat twenty right now?" (There will still be some with their hands raised.)

"What about fifty? (Several will probably still raise their hands.) What would happen if you ate fifty candies right now?" (They might admit that they might get sick; if not, suggest it.)

"Our bodies are a gift from God; how we treat this gift is important. If we mistreat our body, it will fail us. Whether we are dealing with food or sexuality, our physical self is an important part of who we are."

Read aloud, or have someone read aloud, Romans 12:1-2.

Ask: (giving youth the opportunity to answer)

▶ What does it mean to give our body to God?
▶ Why are we asked to live differently than other people?
▶ How does this passage relate to God's gift of our sexuality?

Read from your denomination's ritual for Christian marriage. Expand on the idea of God's plan for us to be in relationship with another to whom we are committed for life.

Invite youth to consider carefully and prayerfully what this information, along with the rest of the content of the experience, means to them. Hand out a "Promise Card" (page 93) to each person. Ask them to consider the promises they would like to make to themselves and to God and to write them on the card. If you are in a sanctuary, invite the youth to use the altar for their prayer time. (Play appropriate music in the background to help create a contemplative mood, or create a "holy setting" by lighting a candle to create a visual focus.)

Close the worship and the experience with a circle of prayer. Remind the youth to take their "Promise Cards" with them and to put them somewhere in their room so that the cards can remind them of the promises they have made. Ask each participant to say a one-word prayer of thanksgiving aloud as you go around the circle. (Anyone may pass to the next if he or she is not comfortable praying in front of others.)

Celebrate
For the last session, it is appropriate for leaders and youth to celebrate the new relationships and information they have experienced. A pizza party, a "shirt signing" (everyone supplies a white T-shirt to be signed by family group members or the total group), and Communion are some ideas for celebrating.

Remind the youth to take their "Promise Cards" with them and to put them somewhere in their room so that the cards can remind them of the promises they have made.

CONTRACEPTIVES CHART

All major contraceptive methods are listed below. Effectiveness rates are based on 100 females having sexual intercourse over the course of a year.

Behind the practical use of contraceptives is the Christian value of love lived out in responsibility, self-control, waiting, and not living in the moment. The consideration of contraceptives means stopping and figuring out what to do to prevent pregnancy and infection.

ABSTINENCE	CONDOM	CONDOM
Saying **no** to sexual intercourse is the only 100%-effective method of birth control.	**Condom** (88% to 98% effective) Placed over the man's penis, condoms prevent pregnancy by stopping sperm from reaching the uterus. When used correctly, latex condoms also can help prevent the spread of STIs.	**Female Condom** (79% to 95% effective) This latex barrier is placed inside the vagina before intercourse.
DIAPHRAGM	**SPERMICIDES**	**INJECTION**
Diaphragm or Cervical Caps (82% to 95% effective) Inserted into the woman's vagina, diaphragms cover the cervix and prevent pregnancy by stopping sperm from reaching the uterus. For maximum effectiveness, the diaphragm or cervical cap should be used with spermicidal jellies, foams, or creams.	**Spermicides** (72% to 97% effective) Contraceptive foams, jellies, creams, and suppositories contain chemical spermicides that, when inserted into the vagina, prevent pregnancy by killing the sperm before they reach the uterus.	**Injection** (99% effective) The birth control shot, administered every three months, contains a hormone that prevents pregnancy.
IMPLANTS	**PILLS**	**IUDS**
Implants (99%+ effective) Implants are flexible, match-sized sticks placed under the skin on the inside of a woman's upper arm. They contain a hormone that prevents pregnancy for five years.	**Pills** (97% to 99% effective) Birth control pills contain hormones that prevent pregnancy. Pills are safe and effective for most women if taken as prescribed.	**IUDs** (97% effective) An intrauterine device is a small, T-shaped plastic piece, that contains either copper or a hormone that prevents pregnancy. A doctor or nurse places it into the uterus.

Let's Be Real: Honest Discussions About Faith and Sexuality

CONTRACEPTIVES CHART

(continued)

FERTILITY AWARENESS	SURGERY	NO METHOD
Fertility Awareness (75% to 97% effective) This means avoiding sexual intercourse during the woman's fertile period, but the fertile time frame may be difficult to determine, especially for an adolescent and is not always reliable because of stress, illness, or use of medicines.	**Surgery** (99%+ effective) A woman may undergo surgery (tubal ligation) to seal off the fallopian tubes. A man may have surgery (vasectomy), in which the vas deferens are sealed, tied, or cut.	**No Method** (15% effective) No protection against pregnancy.
WITHDRAWAL		
Withdrawal (removal of the penis from the vagina just prior to ejaculation) Requires commitment and great control. Least effective and least reliable.		

If a method is 99% effective, 1 woman in 100 having sexual intercourse regularly for one year is expected to become pregnant. If a method is 15% effective, 85 out of 100 women would be expected to become pregnant. Effectiveness is also dependent on the correct and consistent use of the method.

STI INFORMATION SHEET

Sexually Transmitted Infections (STIs) are a class of infections that can be transmitted from an infected person to a sexual partner through close physical and sexual contact. STIs can be prevented. They infect men, women, and children. They can be passed from a pregnant mother to her unborn child. They are not contracted by casual contact or by touching toilet seats or doorknobs. More than 10 million people contract STIs every year. STIs are an epidemic in the 15–24 age group.

► You can have an STI with no outward, physical signs.
► You can have more than one STI at the same time.
► You can get an STI the first time you have sexual intercourse.
► Abstinence is also the safest way to assure that you remain infection free from STIs. It is almost impossible to contract a sexually transmitted infection if you practice abstinence.

Listed below are the most common STIs and the treatments. You can get help and treatment for most STIs without giving your name and without a parent's permission.

GONORRHEA

A bacterial infection that could lead to severe inflammation of the urinary tract and can cause Pelvic Inflammatory Disease (PID) and sterility. Burning during urination, vaginal discharge, fever, stomach pain, and a whitish discharge from the penis are all signs, but there may be no symptoms at all. It can be quickly treated with antibiotics.

SYPHILIS

Caused by a spirochete bacterium, syphilis attacks the nervous system and may lead to paralysis, blindness, insanity, disfiguration, and eventual death. A hard, painless sore, called a *chancre* forms on the penis, vagina, or rectum, one to thirteen weeks after sexual contact. The chancre may disappear; however, the infection continues to grow. This can be treated with antibiotics.

CHLAMYDIA

This is the fastest-spreading STI among young people. It is symptomless until complications flair. It can cause arthritis and sterility if untreated. With an odorless discharge and burning and pain during urination, chlamydia can cause Pelvic Inflammatory Disease in females. Eye, ear, and lung infections can occur in babies. This can be treated with antibiotics.

GENITAL HERPES

Herpes simplex virus type 2 is the usual cause of genital herpes. The infection never leaves the body and can flair at any time. The onset of herpes can be caused by stress, fever, or physical trauma. Symptoms include small, sore clusters on or around the penis, vagina, mouth, and anus. This can be passed to a baby during delivery. Treatment is restricted to topical and oral treatment to help keep the sores dry and clean.

CONDYOMA
(genital warts)

Tiny or larger warts can be flat or shaped like a cauliflower. Warts can appear in the genital area, throat, and anus. The warts can be passed on to a baby during delivery. This can be treated with chemicals such as podophylin, liquid nitrogen, lasers, or conventional surgery.

VAGINITIS

A group of diseases mainly found in the female, but which can be carried and spread by males. Symptoms can include a frothy, yellow or white discharge, itching, burning, and an unpleasant odor. This can be treated with antibiotics.

HIV/AIDS (Human Immunodeficiency Virus/Acquired Immune Deficiency Syndrome)

The most deadly of STIs, the virus destroys the body's immune system. High-risk groups include gay and bisexual men, people who share intravenous needles, and persons engaging in sexual activity with multiple partners or people in this group. After an incubation period of several months to several years, the disease can cause recurring fevers, night sweats, shortness of breath, and a dry cough not related to allergies or smoking. Complicating diseases finally cause death. There is as yet no cure. AZT is one of a series of drugs used to slow the illness.

PUBIC LICE AND SCABIES

Commonly known as "crabs," these bugs live and breed in pubic hair. They are tiny mites that live under the skin of the infected person. Intense itching is the only symptom. They may be passed through linens and clothing. Treatments include Kwell ointment, lotions, shampoos, or A-200 pyrinate.

Let's Be Real: Honest Discussions About Faith and Sexuality

PROMISE CARD

Having spent this time thinking about God's good gift of sexuality, I would like to make the following promises to myself and to God:

I will do my best to live up to these promises by thinking about my responsibilities related to my sexuality, remembering what it means to be a Christian in relation to my sexual expression, and asking God to guide me as I make sexual decisions.

_____
(signature)

YOUTH DEVELOPMENT FIGURE 1

AGE LEVEL	PHYSICAL DEVELOPMENT PSYCHO/ SPIRITUAL	CRITICAL LIFE ISSUES	FAITH DEVELOPMENT ISSUES	PROGRAM IMPLICATIONS
PRE- TEEN Grades 5–6	BEGINNING TO: coordination varies widely enter puberty (girls) desire joining groups spend time with one special friend ABLE TO: identify with sports, media figures conform to rules, expectations	being "good" Fairness is major concept. fear of losing or of being abandoned by parents, friends connecting actions and intentions	beginning to ask religious questions and make commitments learning stories of faith: heroes and heroines What is a Christian?	CAPABLE OF: conforming to rules for reward imitative creating EFFECT learning includes: concrete activities belonging important participation in congregational ministries, story-telling, organized games
EARLY TEEN Grades 7–8	BEGINNING TO: experience sexual relationships be restless and energetic enter puberty (boys) ABLE TO: use variety of thought processes choose what's exciting as what's good identify music style of preference	being separate from parents acceptance by peers, adults loyalty to school, friends physical appearance can be overly critical	Can I trust the faith community? Can I doubt? Is it OK to say no? Grace versus Law What does denomination mean and why is it important?	CAPABLE OF: response learning increased responsibility EFFECT learning includes: exploring service ministries large visual images, multi media active learning warm affection
MID TEEN Grades 9–10	BEGINNING TO: think inductively & deductively make decisions of convenience reflect on family relationships increase strength & coordination ABLE TO: strategize build concepts from facts have increased empathy	employment & related problems style of clothes, hair, food choices	Peers have major decision-making influence. like to look at variety of authorities	CAPABLE OF: choosing from options with rationale EFFECT learning includes: involvement in variety of service ministries variety of learning styles role-plays learning simulations

Let's Be Real: Honest Discussions About Faith and Sexuality

YOUTH DEVELOPMENT FIGURE 1 (continued)

AGE LEVEL	PHYSICAL DEVELOPMENT PSYCHO/ SPIRITUAL	CRITICAL LIFE ISSUES	FAITH DEVELOPMENT ISSUES	PROGRAM IMPLICATIONS
LATE TEEN Grades 11–12	BEGINNING TO: be motivated by abstract ideas admire significant leaders attain maximum height ABLE TO: sense competence as leader initiate projects and programs	college/vocational choices respect for alternative values, lifestyles, customs	less literal faith values rational decisions discipleship beyond high school an emerging concern What's unique about the Christian lifestyle?	CAPABLE OF: relating concepts to concrete situations EFFECT learning includes: giving leadership emphasis on application & appropriation completing unfinished scenarios addressing questions of evil & God's presence

LEARNING SEQUENCE FIGURE 2

AGE LEVEL	BIBLICAL KNOWLEDGE	FAITH DEVELOPMENT KNOWLEDGE	DISCIPLESHIP IMPLICATION KNOWLEDGE	LIFE SKILLS ISSUES KNOWLEDGE
PRE- TEEN Grades 5–6	Specific stories Bible as guide for daily life example of biblical friends learning how to "get around" in the Bible—components	connection between actions and consequences	emphasis on here and now begin building decision-making skills	variety of program activities addressing physical & emotional changes often perfectionists build on interest, enthusiasm
EARLY TEEN Grades 7–8	stories of God's grace rebellion, sin, restoration devotional usage stories of alienation, aloneness images of God's steadfastness Crucifixion & Resurrection narrative	Confirmation introduce responsibility for creation personal devotional life God's grace, forgiveness	begin integrating service options	friendship choices emerging self-consciousness care-giving skills values regarding alcohol & other drugs realities of family life racial/ethnic inclusion sexuality self-image, esteem

AGE LEVEL	BIBLICAL KNOWLEDGE	FAITH DEVELOPMENT KNOWLEDGE	DISCIPLESHIP IMPLICATION KNOWLEDGE	LIFE SKILLS ISSUES KNOWLEDGE
MID TEEN Grades 9–10	life issues & biblical insights covenant community levels of meaning of resurrection atonement passages outreach stories	Confirmation update	exploring meaning and choices	use of autonomy & independence begin leader skills development conflict resolution time usage sexuality planning skills dealing with diversity getting a job
LATE TEEN Grades 11–12	patterns of biblical literature transformational studies related to imagining the future Resurrection as life image historical/critical realities	Confirmation update	vocation as faith expression	advanced leader skill development economic realities & responsibility education choices

Let's Be Real: Honest Discussions About Faith and Sexuality

STUDY GUIDE FOR PARENTS' SESSIONS

These
sessions
are
intended
to be an
hour long.

These sessions are intended to be an hour long. There are six sessions, but you might want to combine some of these. You can use this guide concurrently with the youth sessions, in a retreat setting, or in a church school class or share group.

INTRODUCTORY SESSION: THE MOST IMPORTANT PERSON IN THE ROOM

▶ **Leaders:** Have two leaders, one male and one female, to provide a balance to the presentation.
▶ **Nametags:** As the parents enter the room, have nametags available. It would be fun to make them in the shape of the universal symbols for male and female.
▶ **Leaders:** Introduce yourselves and tell the group the overall purpose for these sessions.
▶ **Purpose:** To understand why the teen is the most important person in the room.
▶ **Openers:** "Share your name and the names of your children. Share briefly where your name came from."

Sharon Adair and **Fred Winslow,** the writers of *Let's Listen,* are the writers of the study guide material in Appendix B.

Bible Openers: Please take all Scripture from the Contemporary English Version. This is the version that will be used with the youth. Say, "You were created by God. God gave us the gift of sexual intercourse. You are the result of that act. Let's read where God gave us that act and called God's creation good."

Read: Genesis 1:26-28, 31

Say: "God gave us our genders, male and female. God gave us the gift of sexual intercourse. In the first chapter of the first book, the Bible talks about our sexuality. We are a creation of God."

Leaders ask: "Where did you first learn about sex in general? Siblings, locker room, slumber party? How old were you, and how did you feel emotionally when you heard the news?" Ask for a show of hands on these questions: "How many learned from parents? from school? from friends? from church? You may raise your hand more than once."

Ask and discuss: "What did you learn? What will you do differently with your teen? In your conversations with your teen, who is the most important person in the room?"

Hand out the Youth Development chart, Appendix A, pages 94–96.

Closing Worship: Stand in a circle, holding hands. Read Genesis 1:26-28, 31a.

Leader closes with prayer: "Dear God, we thank you for the gift of our sexuality. Thank you for creating us. Give us courage to share with our teens. Let each youth be the most important person in the room. Amen."

SESSION 1: MEDIA AND IMAGES OF FAITH

Purpose: To understand media's impact and to develop ways to stand up to it.

Openers: "Share your name and the names of your TV show. Share briefly why it's your favorite. Yes, generally dogs will love *Lassie.*

Bible Openers: Say, "Media often present a false image of what life is really like."

Read: Exodus 20:16-17 from the Contemporary English Version

Say: "Tonight we want to talk about the media's impact on how we view sexuality and sexual expressions. More importantly, we talk about how we can counter those images."

Activity: In the Hunt—Make three posters labeled Negative, Positive, and Sex Sells. Have a magazine (*Time, Newsweek, Glamour, Seventeen, Vogue,* and so forth) for each person. Invite everyone to find six or seven pictures, some that portray a positive image of sexuality, some that portray negative images of sexuality, and some advertisements that use sex to sell.

Post these pictures on the wall under the three posters. Talk about the pictures. Point to a picture and ask, "Why was it put under this category?" Cover up the product on the "Sex Sells" pictures and ask: "Does someone know the product?" Encourage the group to talk about why media uses sexuality, and how the media influences our (and our youth's) decisions.

Closing Worship: Re-read Exodus 20:16-17. As the group sits in a circle, play a Christian CD or tape that demonstrates media can be used for good purposes. God tells the truth in God's Word. Listen to the Word of the Lord.

Closing Prayer: Ask the parents to say "Amen" after each statement, if they agree.

"God give us courage."
"God helps families."
"God loves our teens."
"Let's listen to the word of the Lord."
"Let's listen."

SESSION 2: LISTEN TO YOUR BODY

Purpose: To help parents feel more comfortable with using the anatomically correct terms, and to discuss healthy ways of talking about body parts, rather than veering between lust and shame.

Supplies
▶ Two sets of flash cards with the parts of the sexual anatomy printed on them in bold letters.
▶ Two posterboards. One with the leaders drawing of the female and one with the male. Draw the pictures from LET'S BE REAL, pages 50–52. Do not worry if you do not have a lot of artistic talent. In fact, it will be better for the group if these are less than perfect. The group will have good fun with your drawings and that's OK.

As the parents enter the room, have them again wear nametags. Have them look at pages 50–52. Ask the parents to look at the artist's rendering of the opposite sex and to write a body part on their nametag. Be prepared to place your nametag on the posterboard in the appropriate place.

Openers: Say, "Tell your name and the body part printed on your nametag. Define the body part. Parents may cheat and look in the book for the definition."

Bible Openers: Say, "We veer between lust and shame. Let's listen to the word of the Lord about the God who created us.

Read: Psalm 139:15-16a

Say: "God was present at your conception. Parents talk of the miracle of life when their children are born. They know God has something to do with the giving of life. Because God is involved, we treat the body with respect. Tonight we will have fun learning appropriate ways to talk about the body."

Activity: Body Posters—Put the two drawings of the male and female on the wall. **Say,** "Bring your nametags up and place the nametag next to the body part that is written on your nametag." Make flash cards for the rest of the body parts listed on the drawing, and ask someone to place them on the poster. Say all the body parts out loud as a group.

Closing Worship: Say, "Listen to the word of the Lord. Our body is a temple. Do we treat it like one?" Read 1 Corinthians 6:19.

Closing Prayer: People say "Amen" after each statement if they believe it.

> **Encourage the group to talk about why media uses sexuality, and how the media influences our (and our youth's) decisions.**

Leader: "God gave us feet. We can run, jump, walk, or dance with these feet. Thank God for the gift of feet."

People: "Amen."

Leader: "God gave us hands. We can draw, write, shoot a basket, or hold a lover. Thank you, God, for the gift of hands."

People: "Amen."

"God gave us mouths. We can shout God's praises, whisper sweet nothings, or sing a song. Thank God for the gift of mouths.

People: "Amen."

Leader: "God gave some of us vaginas and some of us penises. We can enjoy sexual pleasure, and we can create life with them. Thank God for the gift of our sex organs."

People: "Amen."

Leader: "God be with us in the embarrassment of using these words in a prayer. God be with us as we move from shame and lust to appreciation for the good gift of our bodies. And the people said...Amen."

Everyone: "Amen."

SESSION 3: WHAT TO DO? POSITIVE CHRISTIAN DECISION-MAKING

Purpose: To roleplay, using parent communication skills that will help parents listen better.

Supplies
▶ A set of flash cards with role-plays outlined on the cards.
▶ Make sure a copy of the parent resource, *Let's Listen,* is available for everyone.

As the parents enter the room, have them wear nametags again. Have them look at "Ten Great Questions to Get Teens to Share More," on page 18 in *Let's Listen*. Ask them to write down one of the "Ten Great Questions" on the back of their nametag.

Openers: Say, "Tell us your name and the "Great Tip to Get Teens to Share More" that you put on the back of your nametag. Tell the group why you think that it will or will not work."

Bible Openers: Let's listen to the word of the Lord, about the Jesus who knows our heart and pushes us to think deeper than ever before.

Read: Matthew 5:27-28 in the the New Revised Standard Version

Ask: "What does Jesus mean by 'has already committed adultery with her in his heart?' " Wait for responses. Close with "Jesus knew lust was a spiritual problem as well as a physical problem."

Activity: Roleplaying—In the roleplay, one of the leaders will play a teenager. Ask a parent to volunteer to roleplay a parent. Draw one of the flash cards. Choose situations for the roleplay from Chapter 3 of the parent resource, such as, "Jessica is a slut. I'd never date her." Use about five situations.

Have the group try roleplaying with the parent asking the usual question or making the usual comment such as, "How do you know that?" Let them roleplay as naturally as they can for a few moments. Generally, the conversation will turn to fact finding. Ask: "Is that helpful? Who is the most important person in the room? Jessica or your teen?"

Have the group roleplay again. This time, have the parent look on their nametag at the "Ten Great Questions to Get Teens to Share More." Ask, "Does the invitation work?" If not, have another parent suggest one that might. Ask, "Now where does the conversation go?" Probably the teen will share more. (Note: Leaders will need to read this chapter thoroughly to understand the method.)

When the roleplaying parent is stuck, ask the group to help out. Usually they will know how to break the log jam. Say, "Don't worry about mistakes. Teens will appreciate your struggle to try to get it right."

Use your other cards and your other "Ten Great Questions." Make sure that you practice "Listening Without Giving In," on page 19 of the parent resource.

Closing Worship: Listen to the word of the Lord. Read Luke 10:25-28. Say, "Jesus knew the answer, but put the conversation back on the lawyer."

SESSION 4: THEY'RE IN TOO DEEP! POSITIVE CHRISTIAN RELATIONSHIPS

Purpose: To explore ways to help your teens value abstinence and virginity.

Supplies
- ▶ Index cards and pencils
- ▶ Large sheets of paper and markers
- ▶ Two real roses, and enough small silk roses for each parent to have one.

As the parents enter the room, have them wear nametags again. Have them write down on the back of their nametag five ways they model good relationships.

Bible Openers: Listen for the Word of God.

Read: John 4:17-18

Say: "The woman at the well appears to fail at relationships over and over. Jesus points out that her current relationship is not within marriage. We want our teens to be successful in their relationships, unlike this woman. Tell us your name and one of your five ways you model good relationships. Tell the group how you think your modeling will help your teen."

> **We want the teen to honor his or her sexuality by keeping it whole and beautiful.**

Activity: Have the group brainstorm ways for their teenager to say No! to sexual intercourse. List these ways on the large sheet of paper. You may want to post it in the room where the youth are attending their sexuality sessions.

Closing Worship: Listen for the word of the Lord. Read 1 Corinthians 12:26. Say, "If we honor our sex organs with virginity and abstinence, then the whole body will be happy."

Use a fresh rose as a symbol of sexuality. Have parents sit in a circle. Pass the rose, having each parent pull a petal off. After all the petals are pulled off, say, "This is a symbol of your teen's sexuality. Your teen may choose to save his or her sexuality and give it to the person he or she plans to spend his or her life with. Or your teen may choose to tear off a petal and give part of their sexuality to every person your teen thinks he or she is in love with. Even if I try to put the petals back, I can't do it. We want the teens to honor their sexuality by keeping it whole and beautiful. But the choice is theirs to honor or to give away. Take a silk rose, and give it to your teen as a reminder of the gift of sexuality."

Pray: "Dear God, thank you for the gift of sexuality. May it be used as the gift it is. Amen."

SESSION 5: WAIT, WAIT, WAIT IT OUT!

Purpose: To help the parent understand teen relationships

Opener: Say, "Wear your nametag and describe your best fantasy date on the back. Then tell the group about your fantasy date."

Activity: Have everyone sit in a circle around one chair. Tell the men: "Pretend that you are a fifteen-year-old teenager again. Tell us what you liked about girls, and what you did not like." Have the men take turns in

Let's Be Real: Honest Discussions About Faith and Sexuality

the center chair, telling their likes and dislikes. (The women are bound to hear something they don't like. Encourage them to get in the chair and tell their likes and dislikes about boys when the women take their turns.)

Bible Reading: Read Exodus 4:10-12. **Say,** "Moses is afraid he won't have the words to say. We are also afraid we won't have the words when we try talking with our teens. But it is in trying that we learn God is with us. God will give us the words to say and the ears to hear with. Trust your faith."

Have each member of the group share one sentence about what they will say to their teen about the teen's sexuality.

Closing Worship: Read the "Conclusion: Final Exam" (*Let's Listen,* page 32) together as a final litany.

Resource List

How to Talk to Your Kids About Really Important Things: Social and Behavioral Science Ser.—For Children Four to Twelve: Specific Questions and Answers and Useful Things to Say, by Charles Schaefer and Theresa Di Geronimo (Jossey Bass).

Parenting With A Purpose: A Positive Approach for Raising Confident, Caring Youth, by Dean Feldmeyer and Eugene C. Roehlkepartain (Search Institute, 1995).

Love and Sex in Plain Language, by Eric W. Johnson (Bantam Books, 1988).

To the Point: AIDS (Abingdon Press, 1993).

The Church Studies Homosexuality, by Dorothy L. Williams (Cokesbury, 1994).

Parents' Introductory Session

For parents of youth participating in the LET'S BE REAL sexuality education course.

Note: If there are parents who do *not* attend the introductory session or the six-week parents' session, *be sure* they receive this information.

Welcome

It is helpful to provide some light refreshments for parents as well as nametags and a comfortable meeting space.

Session Purpose

You may wish to begin with introductions of the leaders for the youth course and give a brief overview of how the decision to implement this course was made.

The purpose of this session is to give a brief overview of the goals of the course and to identify ways that parents can enhance the overall experience.

The purpose of LET'S BE REAL is to help youth, parents, and other significant adults in the church and the community have honest discussions about beliefs, values, and sexuality so that youth have guidance in their faith journey and their decision-making.

The goals of this course include the following:

1. Helping youth gain knowledge and direction concerning their emerging sexuality as growing Christians, members of the faith community, and members of families;
2. Providing faith-oriented helps for decision-making and relationship enhancement;
3. Helping parents support their sons and daughters in making commitments to practice abstinence as a healthy, responsible, and appropriate lifestyle.

Resources

The resources used in this course are

> *LET'S BE REAL: HONEST DISCUSSIONS ABOUT FAITH AND SEXUALITY*
> This is the leader's guide that will provide information and session plans with the youth.

Let's Decide: Faith and My Sexuality
This pocket-sized resource is designed just for youth to read and reflect on the ideas and Scriptures included in the resources. Leaders may choose to use this resource at times during the course.

Let's Listen: Communicating With Your Youth About Faith and Sexuality
This is a guide to help parents learn skills for talking with their youth about sexuality.

Expectations

Say: "This course is designed to emphasize that parents are the primary sexuality educators. For this course to be effective, a parent's involvement may include the following:

▶ Read the parent resource, *Let's Listen,* as a preparation for talking with your youth.
▶ Invest significant interest in listening when your youth return home after the sessions with any questions or concerns. Remember that not every account you hear of what has happened may be completely accurate. Feel free to call the leaders and ask for clarification if you're concerned about what's reported by your youth.
▶ Work with your youth on any assignment given in the learning sessions.
▶ Encourage your youth with positive images of the importance of what they're doing and its lifelong impact on their development.

Dialogue Time

Extend an invitation to parents for their questions about the sexuality course for their youth. The following are some questions they may ask:

1. **Should the church be talking about sex?**
    Yes! Helping youth mature in their awareness of healthy, responsible sexuality affirms God's good gift of sexuality. It's the church's unique role to reclaim the sacredness of sexuality in contrast to the cheap, fictitious images of the media.

2. **What's the course based on?**
    Three basic affirmations are emphasized:

    a. Abstinence as the best choice for Christians;
    b. Affirmation of the strong connection between our sexuality and our faith as disciples of Jesus Christ;
    c. Awareness of the facts necessary for responsible decision-making.

The course challenges the current assumption that abstinence is an unrealistic expectation. The Christian faith community provides resources that can help young people make and keep commitments of sexual abstinence before marriage.

3. How were these resources developed?

The writing team for this course is comprised of parents, pastors, youth ministers, editors, and nationally-known sexuality educators. These writers know the value of good-quality sexuality education for the lives of young people. General editors for this resource are Duane Ewers and Steve Games. They were aided by youth leaders, educators, and pastors who reviewed manuscripts and provided valuable critique and suggestions. Youth in local church and regional events also tested this course and provided candid comments and insightful ways to improve it. We appreciate our partners and their commitment to excellence.

4. What will happen in the sexuality course?

Leaders will have opportunities to adapt the sessions, with special consideration for the maturity and needs of the youth involved. Overall, youth will receive information, participate in creative learning exercises, and have lots of opportunity for reflection and commitment-making.

5. What are the specifics?

Tell parents the specific facts about your course, such as dates, times, and meeting places. This is a great time to articulate specific expectations of parents during the course, such as providing refreshments or other assistance. You may wish to request their commitment to be in prayer for all of the youth as they begin this learning adventure.

If time permits, you may wish to break the group of parents into smaller groupings and ask them to take 5–10 minutes to talk about their feelings and concerns as they support their youth during this course. A few minutes of larger group sharing of their discussions may follow.

The Journey Begins

A closing prayer can lift up the leaders and helpers who will be conducting the course. Prayers can also ask for guidance for parents as well as for the entire congregation as they support this crucial learning time for youth.

Adjournment

Construction of the Male and Female Reproductive Anatomies
(Allow 30 minutes.)

(This exercise is taken from *Streetwise to Sexwise,* by Steve Brown, The Center for Family Life Education, Planned Parenthood of Greater Northern New Jersey, 575 Main Street, Hackensack, NJ, 07601 [201-489-1265], pages 120–121, 128–128.)

Leader's Note
Constructing the reproductive anatomy models can be tricky. It is essential that you become very familiar with how to do it so that you will have no difficulty explaining every step to the group. Practice the processes found on pages 110–115 before attempting them with a group.

Give significant consideration to using this creative learning experience. Are the youth in your group mature enough to follow detailed instructions? Are you comfortable leading this kind of activity? Will parents approve of this kind of activity? Depending on the maturity of your group, you may wish to remove the models from view after the activity.

Supplies
- markers
- adhesive tape
- large sheets of paper
- crayons
- pencils
- construction paper
- photocopies of the male and female reproductive anatomy models (See pages 50–52.)
- supplies for the construction of the male and female reproductive models (Have one set of these supplies for every two people in your family group.)

Supplies for the Male Model
- two 18-inch pieces of rope (Clothesline works well.)
- one 6-inch piece of rope
- one plastic sandwich bag (Do not use the zippered variety.)
- one small, round balloon (uninflated)
- three 6-inch squares of aluminum foil
- clear adhesive tape
- white paper
- scissors

Supplies for the Female Model
- one plastic sandwich bag (Do not use the zippered variety.)
- two flexible drinking straws (Cut from each a 6-inch section from the flexible end.)

- one rubber band
- red yarn
- clear adhesive tape
- two 6-inch squares of aluminum foil
- red tissue paper
- white paper
- scissors

Ask: "Have any of you ever built a model?"

Say: "Today we're going to build models that are a little bit different than what you're used to. We're going to build models of the male and female sexual anatomies."

- Have the participants form pairs.
- Hand out a photocopy of the Male Reproductive Anatomy Model to each pair, or have a large illustration of the model reproduced on a large sheet of paper or on an overhead transparency.
- Have all of the suppies on a table so that each pair can get what they need.
- Demonstrate each step of the process while the pairs work along with you. Make sure that each pair has completed each step correctly before you move on to the next step.

Discussion

Constructing the Male Reproductive Anatomy Model

Supplies
- diagram of completed model
- balloon (bladder)
- aluminum foil (prostate gland)
- 6-inch rope (urethra)
- 18-inch rope (vas deferens)
- rounded ball of aluminum foil (testes)
- 4-inch plastic bag (scrotum)
- paper cutout (penis)

Diagram of the Completed
Male Reproductive Anatomy Model

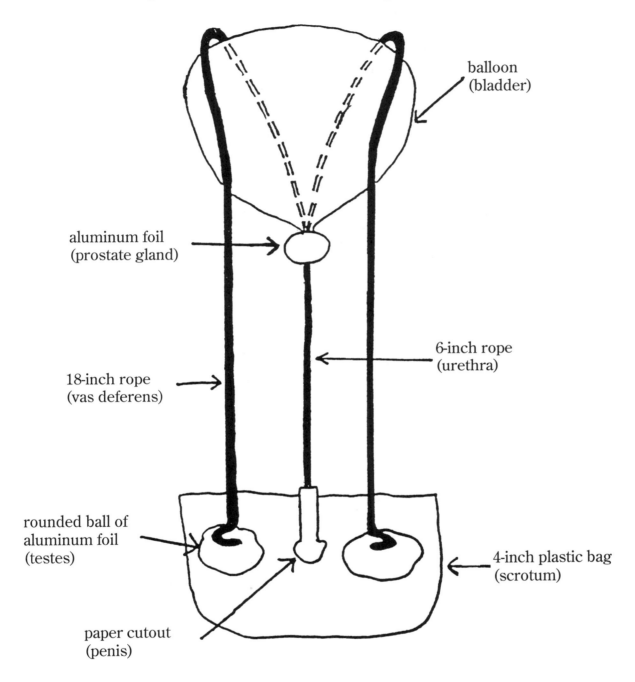

balloon
(bladder)

aluminum foil
(prostate gland)

6-inch rope
(urethra)

18-inch rope
(vas deferens)

rounded ball of
aluminum foil
(testes)

4-inch plastic bag
(scrotum)

paper cutout
(penis)

Appendix D

PART 1

1. Form one piece of aluminum foil into a ball (testicle) and coil one end of an 18-inch piece of rope (vas deferens) around it.

2. Tape the rope to the aluminum foil.

3. Do the same thing with the other 18-inch piece of rope and piece of foil.

4. Join the loose ends of both ropes and tape them together.

5. Slip the plastic bag (scrotum) over the balls of foil and tape the opened end of the bag shut.

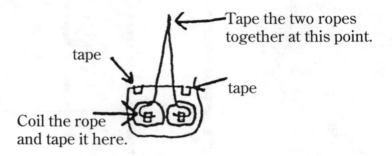

PART 2

1. Blow up the balloon (bladder) to measure about the size of a fist.

2. Tie a knot in the opening of the balloon.

3. Use tape to attach the 6-inch piece of rope (urethra) to the balloon knot.

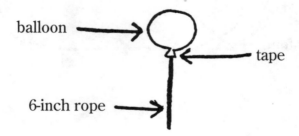

Adapted with permission from Steve Brown's *Streetwise to Sexwise*, Planned Parenthood of Greater Northern New Jersey. For information about this and other related materials, call 201-489-1265.

PART 3

1. Bring the joined ends of the two ropes up over the top of the balloon and down the back.

2. Use tape to attach the longer ropes to the smaller rope at the balloon knot.

3. Tape down the longer ropes at the top of the balloon.

Tape the ropes to the balloon.

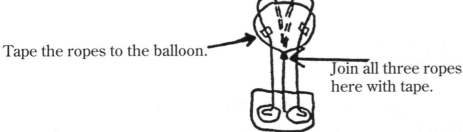

Join all three ropes here with tape.

PART 4

Squeeze the last square of foil around the place where all the ropes come together to form the prostate gland.

Place foil here.

PART 5

1. Trace or copy the patterns below onto white paper.

2. Cut out the tracings and place one on top of the other.

3. Tape the tracings together along both long sides and the rounded end, making sure to leave a small opening (urinary opening) at the tip.

4. Take the taped tracing and pull it over the smaller rope (urethra) to create the penis.

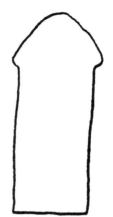

Adapted with permission from Steve Brown's *Streetwise to Sexwise,* Planned Parenthood of Greater Northern New Jersey.
For information about this and other related materials, call 201-489-1265.
Permission to photocopy this page is granted to the purchaser of this publication.

CONSTRUCTING THE FEMALE REPRODUCTIVE
ANATOMY MODEL

Supplies
- ▶ diagram of completed model
- ▶ straw (fallopian tube) with cut ends (fimbriae)
- ▶ sandwich bag (uterus)
- ▶ yarn (endometrium)
- ▶ foil ball (ovary)
- ▶ tape strips (ligament)
- ▶ rubber band (cervix)
- ▶ lower third of plastic bag (vaginal barrel)
- ▶ paper cutout (labia)
- ▶ 1-by-2 eliptical-shaped piece of red tissue paper (hymen)

Diagram of the Completed
Female Reproductive Anatomy Model

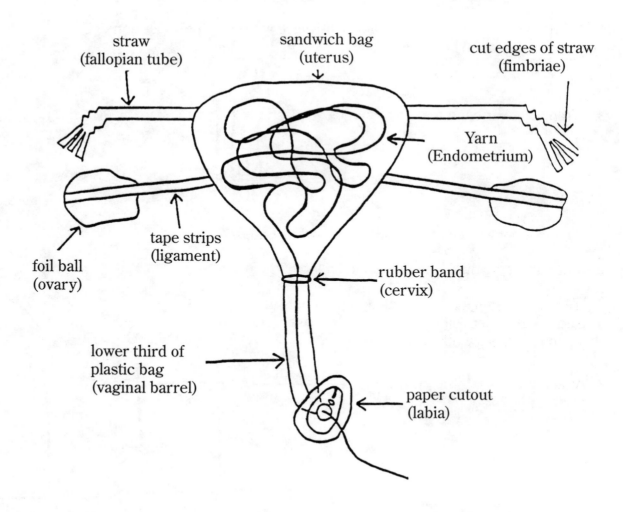

straw (fallopian tube)

sandwich bag (uterus)

cut edges of straw (fimbriae)

Yarn (Endometrium)

foil ball (ovary)

tape strips (ligament)

rubber band (cervix)

lower third of plastic bag (vaginal barrel)

paper cutout (labia)

Adapted with permission from Steve Brown's *Streetwise to Sexwise,* Planned Parenthood of Greater Northern New Jersey. For information about this and other related materials, call 201-489-1265.
Permission to photocopy this page is granted to the purchaser of this publication.

Let's Be Real: Honest Discussions About Faith and Sexuality

PART 1

1. Take a plastic bag (uterus) and cut a very small slit at each side of the bottom.

2. Cut the end of each straw into fringe at the end closest to the flex.

3. Insert the uncut ends of the straws (fallopian tubes) into the slits in the bag and tape them in place.

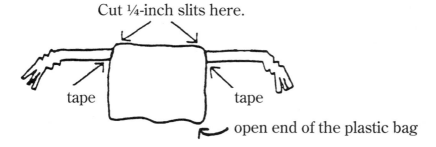

Cut ¼-inch slits here.

tape   tape

open end of the plastic bag

PART 2

1. Place a 36-inch piece of red yarn (endometrium) in the plastic bag and have one end coming out from the bag opening.

2. Wrap a rubber band (cervix) around the plastic bag near the bag opening.

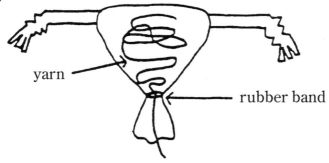

yarn

rubber band

PART 3

1. Squeeze the two squares of foil to make two balls (ovaries).

2. Attach the balls to the plastic bag with strips of tape.

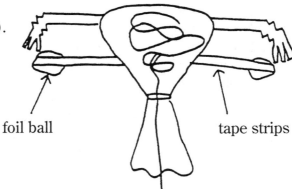

foil ball   tape strips

Adapted with permission from Steve Brown's *Streetwise to Sexwise,* Planned Parenthood of Greater Northern New Jersey.
For information about this and other related materials, call 201-489-1265.

PART 4

1. Trace or copy the outer and inner labia diagrams (see next page) onto white paper.

2. Cut out the tracings and make holes for the urethral and vaginal openings.

3. Place the small, eliptical piece of red tissue paper (hymen) on top of the vaginal opening of the outer labia and tape them together.

4. Place the inner labia on top of the outer labia, line up the holes, and tape the labias together.

5. The clitoris can be drawn on the inner labia with a pencil or marker.

OUTER LABIA

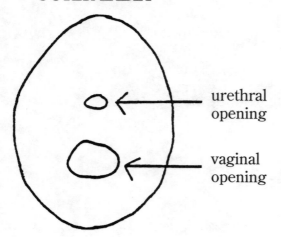

urethral opening

vaginal opening

INNER LABIA

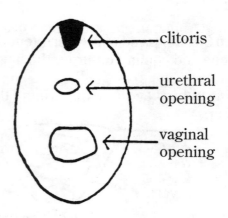

clitoris

urethral opening

vaginal opening

PART FIVE:

To form a complete model, tape the external genitals to the vaginal canal (the open end of the plastic bag), making sure that the urethral opening is uncovered.

Use realistic three-dimensional models, photographs, or drawings (see pages 50–52), and photocopies of the "Reproductive Anatomy: Glossary of Terms" (pages 45–52) to define the process of production, storage, and the journey of sperm from inside to outside the body. In the discussion, you will want to include information about maturation of the male anatomy, erection, and sexual response cycle (see pages 45–48).

Adapted with permission from Steve Brown's *Streetwise to Sexwise,* Planned Parenthood of Greater Northern New Jersey.
For information about this and other related materials, call 201-489-1265.

Let's Be Real: Honest Discussions About Faith and Sexuality

Female Model

Keeping the youth in the same pairs, have the youth construct the female anatomy. Hand out the directions or have a large reproduction of the model on a large sheet of paper or an overhead projector. Demonstrate the process step by step. Be sure that each pair has completed each step before moving on to the next step.

Discussion

Use realistic three-dimensional models, photographs, or drawings and photocopies of the "Reproductive Anatomy: Glossary of Terms" (pages 45–52) to define the process of storage and the journey of the egg.

Ask for volunteers to show the path that the egg travels, starting in the ovary.

Explain the process of conception, what happens to the egg if the egg and sperm come together, and what happens if the egg and sperm do not come together.

Explain that unlike the anatomy of males, a female's sexual anatomy is more hidden. Sometimes females feel that their vagina area (vulva) is dirty and something that shouldn't be touched or talked about. This area is no more dirty that any other part of the body, and it is OK to learn about it. Females can use a mirror to learn about their own vaginal area. Spend time discussing the maturation process and sexual response cycle of the female anatomy (see applicable portions of pages 45–52).

BOOKS

▶ *The What's Happening to My Body? Book for Boys,* by Lynda Madaras, (Newmarket Press, New York, 1991), revised edition, $11.95 (An excellent resource for boys who are going through puberty and for their parents.)
▶ *The What's Happening to my Body? Book for Girls,* (Newmarket Press, New York, 1991), revised edition, $11.95 (An excellent resource for girls who are going through puberty and for their parents.)
▶ *My Body, My Self for Boys: The What's Happening to My Body Workbook,* (Newmarket Press, New York, 1995) $11.95
▶ *My Body, My Self for Girls: The What's Happening to My Body Workbook,* (Newmarket Press, New York, 1995), $11.95
▶ *My Feelings, My Self,* (Newmarket Press, New York, 1993), $11.95
▶ *Get It, Got It, Good! A Guide for Teenagers,* Volume 1, by Carol Noel, (Serious Business, Inc., 1996)

Words You Might Have Heard: A Glossary of Sexual Behaviors

This list of sexual behaviors and orientations was compiled from questions asked by youth.

Abstinence (celibacy)—Not taking part in sexual intercourse.

Anal Sex (copulation)—Penetration of the anus by the penis.

Bisexual—Sexual and emotional attraction to males and females.

Body Image—How a person thinks and feels about his or her body.

Coitus (sexual intercourse)—Sexual union in which the penis enters the vagina.

Cunnilingus ("oral sex")—Using the tongue or mouth to stimulate the female genitalia.

Fellatio ("oral sex")—Using the tongue or mouth to stimulate the male genitalia.

French Kissing—A kiss that uses the tongue within another person's mouth for sexual pleasure.

Group Sex—Sexual activity among more than two people simultaneously.

Heterosexual—Sexual and emotional attraction between a male and a female.

Homosexual—Sexual and emotional attraction between two males (gays) or between two females (lesbians).

Impotence—The inability to have or maintain an erection.

Incest—Sexual activity of any kind between members of the same family.

Masturbation—Self-pleasuring or stimulating one's own genitals to experience sexual excitement or orgasm.

Mutual Masturbation—The simultaneous stimulation of each partner's genitals to produce sexual excitement and orgasm.

Monogamy—Describes a sexually exclusive relationship with one partner only.

Let's Be Real: Honest Discussions About Faith and Sexuality

Oral Sex—Any sexual contact between the mouth and genitals.

Polygamy—Being involved in more than one sexually-active relationship at the same time.

Rape—An act of violence in which sexual activity is forced on one person by another.

Sadomasochism—A sexual orientation and behavior where erotic pleasure is obtained by giving or receiving physical or psychological pain.

Sexual Harassment—Unwelcome and unwanted sexual comments or behavior, repeated often enough to create a hostile environment.

Sexual Self-esteem—How you uniquely look, act, and express yourself as a male or as a female. It is how you value, respect, and regard everything about being you.

Sixty-Nine (69)—A slang term for mutual oral-genital sexual activity. It describes the position the bodies are in, as it resembles the number 69.

Sodomy—Legally, sodomy is sexual activity that involves oral-genital, anal-oral, or anal-genital contact.

Transsexual—A person who believes he or she is really a member of the opposite sex. Some transsexuals undergo a sex-change operation.

Transvestite—A man who gains erotic enjoyment from dressing in female clothing.

Vaginal-Manual Intercourse—A sexual act involving placing a hand in the vagina.

Virgin—A male or female who has never had sexual intercourse. Secondary Virginity is a current term that refers to someone who has been sexually active and who is now making a choice to abstain from sexual intercourse.

OTHER RESOURCES ON HARASSMENT AND RAPE

Everything You need to Know about Sexual Harassment, by Elizabeth Bonchard (The Need to Know Library, 1997; Grades 7–12)

Sexual Harassment: A Question of Power, JoAnn B. Guernsey (Lerner Group, 1995; Grades 6 and up)

Working Together Against Sexual Harassment, by Rhoda McFarland (Rosen Publishing Group, 1996; Grades 7–12)

Sexual Harassment: What Teens Should Know, by Carol Nash, (Enslow Publishers, Inc., 1996; Grades 6 and up, ages 11–18)

Dating: A Peer Education Manual for Reducing Sexual Harassment and Violence Among Secondary Students, by Toby Simon and Bethany Golden (Dating: Learning Publications, 1996; Grades 7–12)

The following publications contain valuable information on rape and dating:

Everything You Need to Know When you are the Male Survivor of Rape or Sexual Assault, by John LaValle (The Need to Know Library, Inc., 1996; Grades 7–12)

Drugs and Rape, by Maryann Miller, (Rosen Publishing Group, 1995; Grades 7–12)

Coping with Date Rape and Acquaintance Rape, by Andrea Parrot, (Rosen Publishing Co., 1993; Grades 7–12)

Working Together Against Violence Against Women, by Aliza Sherman (Library of Social Activism, 1996; Grades 7–12)

Staying Safe on Dates, by Donna Chaiet (Rosen Publishing Group, 1995; Grades 7–12)

Date Abuse, by Herma Silverstein (Enslow Publishers, 1994; Grades 6 and up)

THE CONSULTANTS

Michael Ratliff is an ordained deacon, working as Pastor With Youth at St. Andrew United Methodist Church in Littleton, Colorado. Certified as a Minister of Youth and Minister of Education in The United Methodist Church, Mike worked with the sexuality program in the Florida Conference for seven years. He co-wrote the curriculum adopted as the official sexuality curriculum for the North Georgia Conference. Mike has been involved in local church youth ministry for over twenty-five years, leads workshops on Youth Ministry, recently taught Youth Ministry at Iliff School of Theology, has written for various publications, and has self-published several resources for youth ministry.

The Reverend Diana Anderson Northcutt was born in La Junta, Colorado. She graduated from Southwest Missouri State University with a degree in Social Work and a minor in Religious Studies in 1986; Oklahoma City University with a Masters of Arts in Religion in 1990; and Phillips Theological Seminary with a Masters of Divinity in 1995. Academic honors include Alpha Delta Mu and Omicron Delta Kappa. Professional memberships within the church include Christian Educators Fellowship and Forum of Adults in Ministry with Youth. She is certified in The United Methodist Church as Minister of Christian Education and Youth. Diana has served as a youth minister for over twenty years. She chaired the Human Sexuality Ministries of the Oklahoma Conference, an ecumenical ministry, for eight years, and currently serves a three-point charge at Granite, Carter, and Willow in Southwest Oklahoma. For the past six years she has served as the adult co-chair to the Conference Council on Youth Ministries for the Oklahoma Conference of The United Methodist Church.

Let's Be Real: Honest Discussions About Faith and Sexuality